T0339549

Cambridge Elements ≡

Elements in Business Strategy
edited by
J.-C. Spender
Kozminski University

BUSINESS MODEL INNOVATION

Strategic and Organizational Issues for Established Firms

Constantinos Markides
London Business School

Shaftesbury Road, Cambridge CB2 8EA, United Kingdom

One Liberty Plaza, 20th Floor, New York, NY 10006, USA

477 Williamstown Road, Port Melbourne, VIC 3207, Australia

314–321, 3rd Floor, Plot 3, Splendor Forum, Jasola District Centre, New Delhi – 110025, India

103 Penang Road, #05–06/07, Visioncrest Commercial, Singapore 238467

Cambridge University Press is part of Cambridge University Press & Assessment, a department of the University of Cambridge.

We share the University's mission to contribute to society through the pursuit of education, learning and research at the highest international levels of excellence.

www.cambridge.org
Information on this title: www.cambridge.org/9781108995054

DOI: 10.1017/9781108993241

First published 2023

A catalogue record for this publication is available from the British Library.

ISBN 978-1-108-99505-4 Paperback
ISSN 2515-0693 (online)
ISSN 2515-0685 (print)

Business Model Innovation

Strategic and Organizational Issues for Established Firms

Elements in Business Strategy

DOI: 10.1017/9781108993241
First published online: May 2023

Constantinos Markides
London Business School

Author for correspondence: Constantinos Markides, cmarkides@london.edu

Abstract: Digital technologies have allowed for the proliferation of new business models, something that has attracted the attention of academic research. Much of this research has focused on (i) understanding what a business model is and its theoretical connection to the concept of strategy, and (ii) exploring what business model innovation is and what its sources and outcomes are. Less work has gone into studying the issues that established firms face in business model innovation – such as how to respond to the arrival of a disruptive business model in one's industry, or how to compete with dual business models or how to migrate from one business model to another. This Element approaches the topic of business model innovation from the perspective of the established firm and examines the unique strategic and organizational issues that big, established companies face when a new business model enters their markets.

Keywords: business model innovation, disruption, disruptive innovation, strategy, ambidexterity

ISBNs: 9781108995054 (PB), 9781108993241 (OC)
ISSNs: 2515-0693 (online), 2515-0685 (print)

Contents

Introduction

In the last fifteen years, a voluminous literature has developed around the concept of *business model* (BM). The growing literature has explored various definitions of what a business model is, developed typologies of the most frequently used business models, examined the theoretical foundations of the new concept, examined how the business model concept relates to the Strategy concept and explored how new business models emerge (e.g. Afuah and Tucci, 2001; Amit and Zott, 2001, 2021; Casadesus-Masanell and Ricart, 2010; Chesbrough, 2007 and 2010; DaSilva and Trkman, 2014; Foss and Saebi, 2015; 2017; Magretta, 2002; Markides, 2006; Massa and Tucci, 2013; McGrath, 2010; Spieth, Schneckenberg and Ricart, 2014; Teece, 2010; Zott and Amit, 2007 and 2010; Zott, Amit and Massa, 2011).

Developing in parallel to this literature is a body of research on the concept of *Business Model Innovation* (BMI), a topic related to but distinct from BM. This literature has explored a variety of topics, including the definition of BMI, its antecedents and outcomes, the contingencies that influence its impact, the methodologies that firms can use to discover new innovative business models and the challenge of responding to new business models such as migrating from one to another or competing with dual business models in the same industry (Amit and Zott, 2012; Foss and Saebi, 2017; Johnson and Lafley, 2010; Johnson, Christensen and Kagermann, 2008; Markides, 2006 and 2013; Markides and Oyon, 2010; Massa and Tucci, 2013; McGrath, 2010; Mitchell and Coles, 2004; Ramdani and Boukrami, 2019; Spieth, Schneckenberg and Ricart, 2014). While BM and BMI are obviously related, this Element will focus on the topic of business model innovation.

The literature on BMI has made great strides in the last ten years by using entrepreneurial firms as its primary empirical setting (Foss and Saebi, 2017, p. 214). This focus has meant that the issues explored have been primarily issues important to start-up firms – such as the ways in which a firm can discover a new business model and the dynamic capabilities required to scale up the new business model. This is understandable – most new business models, especially new-to-the-world ones, have been introduced by start-up firms. For example, it is start-up firms such as Uber, Airbnb, Rent the Runway, Ebay, Netflix, Facebook, Amazon, Google, Southwest, IKEA, Nucor and Wikipedia that have revolutionized their respective industries with new and disruptive business models. As a result of this emphasis on the *discovery* of new business models, the research questions explored so far by the BMI literature have focused on issues that are particularly relevant to entrepreneurship rather than big, established firms.

Needless to say, business model innovation is relevant and important for established firms as well. Unfortunately, the insights and knowledge developed thus far by the literature are not particularly relevant to established firms for two reasons: (i) established firms may face the same challenges as start-up firms – such as how to discover or how to scale up a new business model – but since they operate in a different context and face different realities, the answers to these challenges may be different from the answers of the same challenges for start-up firms; and (ii) established firms face additional challenges that start-up firms do not face – for example, how to operate their existing business model while adopting a new (and often disruptive) business model at the same time, or how to migrate from their existing business model to a new one.

The purpose of this manuscript is to bring together the existing knowledge and research on the *unique* issues that *established* firms face when it comes to business model innovation. For example, we know that new business models often 'conflict' with the business models of the established firms (Porter, 1996) and the new markets they create often cannibalize (Christensen, 1997) or undermine the core market – and that's why we call them 'disruptive'! The new business models created by BMI might, for example, replace the existing distributors of the established firm or dilute its existing brands. In addition, they often lead to the creation of new markets that cannibalize the core business of the established firm. And they always compete for resources that come at the expense of the core business. As a result of all these trade-offs and conflicts, the managers of the core business will most likely oppose the discovery or adoption of the new business model – and can sometimes go as far as to actively undermine them. There is now plenty of evidence in the literature that substantiates such a claim (e.g. Khanagha et al., 2013; Markides and Oyon, 2000). We need to acknowledge these facts and appreciate that simply encouraging established firms to 'innovate' and discover new business models will not normally succeed, even when we give them the tools and methodologies on how to innovate. The problem for established firms when it comes to innovating with a new business model is not knowledge but organizational politics and the incentives affecting the behaviors of their leaders. Yes, there are exceptions to this, and yes, there is no doubt that business model innovation can be a source of growth for established firms as well – witness the benefits to Nestlé of developing and growing the Nespresso business model – but the incentives in big firms are such that very few established firms will heed our advice to 'innovate' and discover new business models.

This is not as bad as it sounds! Innovation is not one thing but two: discovery of something new and then scaling it up. Start-up firms may be good at discovery, but big, established firms are good at scaling up. Therefore, it is not all doom and gloom if the big firm does not *discover* new business models. They could still benefit from this type of innovation by 'exploiting' the discoveries of others.

There are several ways in which an established firm can exploit a new business model introduced by entrepreneurial firms in its industry, and our aim is to examine each one and identify the challenges associated with each.

This Element will synthesize what we know from academic research on the issues that established firms uniquely face when it comes to business model innovation. A few of these insights come from my own research over the past twenty years, but obviously, I will also bring into the discussion the ideas and findings of other academics who have been working on these issues.

1 What Is Business Model Innovation?

There is no agreement in the strategy literature as to what a BMI is. In their review of the extant BMI literature, Foss and Saebi (2017: 209) lament the fact that there is a deep ambiguity with respect to what a BMI is and complain that 'Definitions abound, and many of those definitions lack specificity.' There appear to be differences in opinion about every aspect of the BMI concept. For example, could changes in a single component of a BM constitute BMI (Amit and Zott, 2021; Giesen et al., 2007; Schneider and Spieth, 2013) or do we need a change in the whole architecture of a BM (Markides, 2008; Teece, 2010) to consider this a BMI? Similarly, does something qualify as an innovation if it's only new to the firm (Amit and Zott, 2021; Bock et al., 2012) or should it meet the higher standard of being new to the industry or new to the world (Santos, Spector and Van der Heyden, 2009)? There's even disagreement as to whether BMI can be seen as a process or an outcome (Bucherer, Eisert and Gassmann, 2012; Demil and Lecocq, 2010; Doz and Kosonen, 2010; Gunzel and Holm, 2013; Johnson and Lafley, 2010; Mitchell and Coles, 2004).

To make progress in this Element, we need to have a definition, and the one we will utilize is that business model innovation is the discovery of a new business model that is either *new to the world* or *new to the industry* in which it is being introduced. As Amit and Zott (2021) and Foss and Saebi (2017) indicate, there are several other possible definitions that one could adopt, but we pick this one and we will explain why later in this section. However, simple as it might look, this definition needs further clarification, in particular by asking 'What exactly is a business model?' and 'What is new?' We proceed by providing answers to these questions.

What Is a Business Model?

There is still no consensus in the literature on the definition of the business model concept (Foss and Saebi, 2017; Schneider and Spieth, 2013). For example, Amit and Zott (2001: 511) defined it as 'the content, structure and governance of transactions designed so as to create value through the exploitation of opportunities'. By contrast, Baden-Fuller and Morgan (2010) and Baden-Fuller and Mangematin (2013) have encouraged us to view business models not as descriptions of what a firm does but as models of the world that 'go beyond explaining what has happened in a particular context to providing a configuration of cause-effect relations' (Baden-Fuller and Mangematin, 2013: 419). Similarly, Arend (2013) proposed that we should view the business model as a 'model' of value creation, especially involving non-monetary exchanges. In a survey of the literature, Zott, Amit and Massa (2011) found an alarming number of definitions being used, which led them to argue that 'this lack of definitional clarity represents a potential source of confusion, promoting dispersion rather than convergence of perspectives and obstructing cumulative research progress on business models' (Zott, Amit and Massa, 2011: 1023).

Amidst this lack of definitional clarity, there is one definition that has gained widespread acceptance among strategy scholars. This is the definition that looks at the business model as an activity system, more precisely as *a system of interdependent activities* (e.g. Afuah, 2003; Amit and Zott, 2021; Casadesus-Masanell and Ricart, 2010; Hedman and Kalling, 2003; Markides, 2008; Seddon et al., 2004; Teece, 2010; Zott and Amit, 2010; Zott, Amit and Massa, 2011). Having said this, there is still quite a lot of disagreement as to what specific activities make up the business model. For example, an early definition of the business model provided by Slywotzky (1996) and Slywotzky and Morrison (2002) argued that a business model is the collection of choices that a firm makes on *eleven* different dimensions – including its choice of customers and its choice of value capture. By contrast, Hambrick and Fredrickson (2005) identified five key components that make up the business model; Gassmann, Frankenberger and Csik (2020) argued for four ingredients; Mitchell and Coles (2003: 3) provided a definition that included six main elements, namely 'the who, what, when, where, why and how much a company uses to provide its goods and services and receive value for its efforts'; and Amit and Zott (2021) provided a definition that included four key elements, namely the Who, What, How and Why of the business. The only area where there is agreement is that all these activities that make up the business model – whether three or six or eleven – are interconnected. They must, therefore, be put together in a way that they fit into a coherent and self-reinforcing system or architecture (Afuah, 2003; Casadesus-Masanell and Ricart, 2010; Teece, 2010; Zott and Amit, 2010; Zott, Amit and Massa, 2011).

In my earlier work (Markides 1997; 1999; 2008), I defined the business model as a system of *three* key interdependent activities – *who* to target as customers, *what* to offer these customers and *how* to serve these customers, that is, what value-chain activities to put in place to allow the firm to deliver value to these customers in an efficient manner. This definition is nothing more than the Who-What-How framework first introduced in the strategy literature by Abell (1980). It is consistent with the established view that a business model is an activity system and includes most of the other dimensions of a business model that other researchers have put forward. I will therefore use it as the basis to discuss business model innovation in this Element.

Is a Business Model the Same as Strategy?

One of the first questions to emerge in the literature is whether the BM concept is new or whether it is the same as the concept of strategy. For example, Teece (2010: 174) argued that 'the concept of business model has no established theoretical grounding in economics or in business studies'. Similarly, Arend (2013: 390) complained that 'the use of the term "business model" as a "description" of how a traditional venture operates is strong on redundancy and weak on theoretical grounding'. He further argued (Arend, 2013: 392) that 'on one (extreme) hand, it could be argued that the idea of the business model has been yet another un-needed, re-labeled, re-interpretation of the profit equation in search of some distinction as a new level of analysis'. Porter (2001: 73) went as far as to argue that the business model concept is 'an invitation for faulty thinking and self-delusion'.

Despite the criticism and the lack of universally agreed definitions for strategy and business model, there is an emerging consensus that the two concepts are theoretically distinct (e.g. Amit and Zott, 2021; Casadesus-Masanell and Ricart, 2010; Lanzolla and Markides, 2021; Teece, 2010). Specifically, there are two areas where the extant literature points to theoretical differences.

First, strategy has been conceived as the high-level choices that a firm makes – such as *positioning* choices (e.g. should the firm follow a low-cost or a differentiation strategy); *entry timing* choices (e.g. should we be first-mover in a new market or a late entrant); *mode of entry* choices (acquisition versus organic); *industry scope* choices (broad versus narrow); *diversification* choices (related versus unrelated); *geographical* choices (local versus international); and so on. By contrast, a business model has been defined as *the configuration of activities* that a firm puts together to translate its strategy into action. Specifically, the business model is seen as an activity system made up of a number of interdependent activities such as the firm's value-chain activities, its choice of customers and its choice of products and services (e.g. Afuah, 2003; Casadesus-Masanell and Ricart, 2010; Hedman and Kalling, 2003; Markides, 2008; Seddon et al., 2004; Teece, 2010; Zott and Amit, 2010; Zott, Amit and Massa, 2011). The right choice of interdependent activities determines the performance of the system. From this perspective, the business model is the translation of the firm's strategy into the detailed activities it needs to put in place to implement its strategy.

As an illustration of the difference between the two concepts, consider a company like Southwest. The *strategy* of Southwest is to be a point-to-point, low-cost, no-frills airline operator in the southwestern United States (not Europe or Asia). Its *business model*, on the other hand, is the collection of activities that it has put together to execute this strategy – activities such as low-priced tickets, a standardized fleet of aircraft, limited use of travel agents, flying to secondary airports in mid-sized cities in the United States, no food or drinks on board, no baggage transfers, high aircraft utilization and so on.

The second main difference between the two constructs that has been highlighted in the literature is the notion of *interrelatedness* between the activities that make up a business model. Much more important than deciding on what activities to perform, a firm must find a way of combining these activities into *a system* that creates the requisite fit between what the environment needs and what the company does. It is the combining of the activities into a well-balanced system that's important, not the development of individual activities. As Porter (1996: 70) argued: 'strategy is about *combining* activities'. Teece (2010: 180) put it like this: 'The various elements need to be cospecialized to each other and work together well as a system.'

Does the BM Concept Add Anything to Strategy?

For these two reasons, it is therefore possible to make the case that the two concepts are theoretically distinct. However, even if this is the case, the question that still remains is 'Do we gain anything by making this distinction? How does this distinction contribute to the field of strategy?' This has been the subject of much debate in the literature (e.g. Bigelow and Barney, 2021; Lanzolla and Markides, 2021) and the truth is that we still have not converged on a common answer. However, for the purposes of this Element on BMI, there are at least four areas where the distinction between the two concepts can lead to useful insights.

First, the BM concept can help explain performance variation in firms that follow the *same* high-level strategy. Consider, for example, the well-known story of Xerox versus Canon in the copier market. Xerox pioneered the market, but a number of firms, including IBM, Kodak and Canon, followed Xerox into the market as second-movers. Yet, despite following the same strategy (i.e. the second-mover strategy), IBM and Kodak failed to make significant inroads in the market whereas Canon did so successfully. What could explain the difference? There are many possible reasons that differentiate success from failure, but several researchers have suggested that one of these reasons is the different business models that the various players brought into the fight (e.g. Markides, 1997; Porter, 1985). Specifically, IBM and Kodak imitated the main elements of Xerox's successful business model by targeting big corporations as customers; selling their machines on the value proposition of speed of copying; and using their direct sales force to reach the customers. By contrast, Canon targeted small and medium-sized enterprises, sold its machines on the value proposition of cost and quality and distributed its products through its existing dealer network. All firms followed the same high-level strategy (i.e. second mover), but how they chose to operationalize that strategy – the business model – was different, and this made all the difference. This example suggests that the *same* strategy can be translated into action through *different* business models and what determines success is not so much the strategy as the specific business model that has been chosen to convert the strategy into action. Canon chose the 'right' business model. IBM and Kodak did not.

The same point can be seen when we examine other firms that enjoy different degrees of success despite following the same high-level strategy. For example, there are established companies from the same industry that responded to the invasion of a disruptive business model in their market by adopting the same strategy – such as creating a separate unit to house the new disruptive business model. Yet some have failed miserably (e.g. KLM, BA, United, Continental) while others have done so successfully (e.g. Singapore Air, Qantas). Similarly, we have companies that follow the same 'differentiation' (or 'low-cost') strategy in the same industry – yet some are successful, and some are not. In all these cases, to truly understand why some firms succeed while others fail despite following the same strategy, we need to go beyond the high-level strategies and examine in detail the specific business models that firms utilize to give life to their strategy.

This is important for the field of Strategy because any attempts to explain the relationship between a certain strategy (say the 'differentiation' strategy) and the performance of the firm will be biased unless we specifically control for the business model used to translate the differentiation strategy into action. More generally, any econometric equation that aims to explain the performance of a firm as a function of a set of independent variables must control for any variable that influences *both* the dependent and independent variables. In this specific case, the firm's chosen business model influences both the dependent variable (firm performance) and the independent variable (its strategy, such as 'differentiation'). This implies that any examination of the correlation between performance and differentiation must explicitly control for the business models of the firms following a differentiation strategy. Failure to do so will produce a biased estimate of the correlation between performance and differentiation.

This problem can be seen clearly in the voluminous literature on first-mover advantages (FMAs). Despite the strong theoretical arguments supporting the existence of FMAs and despite numerous papers exploring the conditions under which pioneering is a superior strategy, the empirical evidence is rather mixed. As already shown by Vanderwerf and Mahon (1997), a possible reason for the conflicting empirical results may be the methodology used to study FMAs. But as argued here and by Markides and Sosa (2013), another possible reason may be the fact that past studies failed to explicitly control for the business models used by both the pioneer and the late entrants. Failure to do so will produce a biased estimate of the correlation between performance and FMAs.

Although researchers tend to shy away from incorporating the business model variable in their work on the basis that we do not have a clear definition of what a business model is, nothing could be further from the truth. Several useful definitions of business models exist and can be constructively used in our research. It is only by explicitly incorporating this concept in our work that research on the link between strategy and performance can take a leap forward.

The second area where the business model concept can enrich the Strategy literature is by introducing a new source of competitive advantage for a firm – namely the existence of 'conflicts' between one business model and another (Lanzolla and Markides, 2021). In its early days, the Strategy field emphasized industry structure as a source of competitive advantage – things like entry barriers and mobility barriers. With the emergence of the resource-based view of the firm, resources took centre stage as things that can help a firm achieve competitive advantage – especially resources that are valuable, rare and difficult to imitate, replicate or substitute (Barney 1986 and 2001; Wernerfelt, 1984). Porter (1996) introduced the notion of strategy as a system of interrelated activities and this gave rise to yet another possible source of competitive advantage – the sheer number of activities that make the system and the complexity of putting them all together in a coherent and internally consistent whole (Porter and Siggelkow, 2008; Rivkin, 2000; Rivkin and Siggelkow, 2003; Siggelkow, 2001).

By looking at strategy through the lens of business models, a new source of competitive advantage emerges. This is the presence of 'conflicts' between the business models of different industry players. By conflicts we mean that a given business model may require value-chain activities different from and often *incompatible* with those from another business model (Porter, 1980, 1996). For example, an online brokerage business model may alienate the brokers of a firm that is using a traditional business model. This would make response to or competition with the online business model difficult for the traditional competitor. Similarly, the low-cost, point-to-point business model of flying can potentially cannibalize the customer base of a company using the traditional, hub-and-spoke business model of flying, again making response difficult.

The existence of such trade-offs and conflicts means that a company that adopts a business model that contains *many* and *serious* conflicts with the business models of its competitors will establish a competitive advantage over them. The important point to note is that *not* all new business models are equally disruptive. There are different *types* of conflicts (e.g. cannibalization, distribution, culture, incentives, attitudes) as well as different *degrees* of conflict (i.e.

minor versus major). This means that a given business model may be more (or less) disruptive than another business model. This, in turn, implies that a firm could choose to build its competitive advantage *by designing a business model that conflicts in a major way with the business models of its competitors*. The more and bigger the conflicts, the bigger the competitive advantage the firm gains. This has serious implications for how firms ought to engage in the development of their strategies. A key question that must be asked in any strategy development workshop should be 'Can I design the activities of my strategy in ways that conflict with the activities of my competitors' strategies?'

A third area where the business model concept enriches the Strategy literature is in helping us appreciate and then exploit a new type of innovation – specifically business model innovation. This is different from product, or process, or technological innovation and can be the basis for enormous growth even when other types of innovation are not effective. Consider, for example, Enterprise Rent-a-Car, the biggest car rental company in North America. Rather than target travellers as its customers (like Hertz and Avis did), Enterprise focused on the replacement market (i.e. customers who had an accident). Rather than operate out of airports, it located its offices in downtown areas. Rather than use travel agents to push its services to the end consumers, it uses insurance companies and body shop mechanics. Rather than wait for the customer to pick up the rental, it brings the customer to the car. In short, Enterprise built a business model that is fundamentally different from the ones utilized by its biggest competitors. This allowed it to start out in 1957 as a new start-up firm in the industry and grow into the biggest competitor in less than fifty years.

The generalization that emerges from such an example is that late entrants can overcome the FMAs enjoyed by incumbents and succeed in attacking them by utilizing an innovative business model – one that undermines the very FMAs on which incumbents rely. If, for example, Unilever enjoys control of the supermarket shelf by virtue of being an early mover, a late entrant can undermine this FMA by adopting a business model that uses online distribution as one of its key components. Similarly, if British Airways enjoys control of airport gates by virtue of being an early mover, a late entrant can neutralize this FMA by adopting a business model that utilizes alternative airports for its operations. The more general point is that compared to product or process innovations, business model innovation is a fundamentally different type of innovation, with its own characteristics and dynamics. It is another weapon in a firm's arsenal in its competitive battles. Learning how to use it can bring a firm competitive advantage and success.

The fourth and final area where the business model concept can enrich the strategy literature is by emphasizing the importance of value creation (as opposed to value transfer) as a source of profitability. Traditionally, the Strategy literature had been preoccupied with identifying the means through which a firm could improve its performance. Little attention was paid to whether the means through which a firm improved its performance were also enlarging the overall economic pie or not. The business model concept can help us focus the attention of future research on whether this is the reason for a firm's superior performance.

What the existing literature has shown is that business model innovation could enlarge the economic pie in two distinct ways. First, new business models that enter established markets grow *not* only by stealing customers from the established firms but also – and more importantly – by attracting *new* customers into the market (Gilbert, 2003). In fact, as demonstrated by Christensen (1997) and Gilbert and Bower (2002), it is *new* customers that originally get attracted to the invading business model and give it the initial support that it needs to grow. It is only over time that established customers switch to the new thing. This is an important point because it suggests that new business models are not only threats to defend against but also opportunities to exploit (Gilbert, 2003). By enlarging the potential pool of customers, business model innovation allows for more profits to be made by all industry participants. Enlargement of the market is especially evident when the business model innovation is based on (low) prices. We can see such an enlargement of markets in a number of industries that faced business model innovation, such as the airline, banking and steel industries (e.g. Casadesus-Masanell and Ricart, 2010; Christensen, 1997; Gilbert, 2003).

Second, *some* business model innovations will not be based on lower prices but on offering the customers different benefits and different value propositions. For example, the luxury-goods industry has grown enormously on the basis of offering customers emotional benefits rather than functionality (Slywotzky and Morrison, 2002). Similarly, companies such as Starbucks, Swatch and Apple have enlarged their respective markets by introducing new and different benefits to their product offerings (Christensen and Raynor, 2003; Hamel, 1996; Kim and Mauborgne, 2005; Markides 1997). Such innovation allows firms to compete for customers on the basis of differentiation rather than just price. They are value enhancing in that they offer the existing customers more benefits or benefits for which they are willing to pay higher prices.

The potential to enlarge the existing economic pie will vary by business model. For example, Markides, Larsen and Gary (2020) showed that the more radical the BMI, and the more activities in the BM that were being innovated, the bigger the size of the enlargement of the economic pie. They also identified a number of other factors – over and above the nature of the BMI – that influenced how much the economic pie could be enlarged through BMI.

These factors included the maturity of the industry, the number of firms engaged in BMI and the ease and speed with which firms could imitate each other in an industry. It is up to future research to identify the circumstances and the types of business models that lead to more pronounced value creation.

What Is Business Model *Innovation*?

If we start from the premise that a business model is an activity system that combines the Who-What-How decisions of the firm, then business model innovation is the discovery of a new Who-What-How *combination* in a given industry. Note that to qualify as a BMI, it is not enough to just change one or a few of the activities in the system, as other researchers have argued (Amit and Zott, 2021). For example, identifying a new customer or introducing a new inventory system or a new distribution channel will not qualify as BMI. What we want is a fundamental change in the *combination* of the Who-What-How system or, as Teece (2010) suggested, in the *architecture of the system* or the architecture linking the various elements or activities of the system. In that sense, we can have BMI even if none of the existing activities in the system change in any meaningful way. Business Model Innovation is a new *system* that combines either the existing activities or a set of different activities.

This brings us to the thorny issue of what is 'new'. As already argued, a new business model can be new to the firm; or new to the industry; or new to the world (Foss and Saebi, 2017). Table 1 provides a few examples for each category. There is obviously a difference in how radical the innovation is, and this raises the following question: 'Should we treat all three as one and the same and/or should all three be called business model innovations?' For example, Microsoft under its CEO Satya Nadella changed its business model and adopted a subscription model for its suite of Office applications. This is obviously a new business model for Microsoft, but it can hardly be considered a business model innovation like the ones introduced by Amazon, Uber and Airbnb, all of which are business models that are new to the world (or at least, new to the industry). Similarly, motivated by the success of Netflix, companies such as Rent-the-Runway and Perlego introduced the Netflix business model in their respective industries – renting clothes and renting academic textbooks (online) respectively. Again, these are innovations that are new to these industries, but since they are imitating Netflix, they cannot be considered as new-to-the-world innovations. Should they be treated the same as innovations that are new to the world, and should we even call them business model *innovations*? Are they truly innovations if somebody else has already introduced them in another context?

Table 1 Business model innovations

Companies that introduced new-to-the-firm business models	Companies that introduced new-to-the-world or new-to-the-industry business models
Microsoft	Uber
AutoTrader	Netflix
SKY	Airbnb
New York Times	Southwest
Adobe	eBay
Walmart	Dell
John Deere	Rent-the-Runway
BNP Paribas	Amazon
Pearson	Zipcar
Qantas	Expedia
Hilti	Perlego
Barnes and Noble	Facebook
Funda	Wikipedia

From an academic perspective, treating all three types of innovation as one and the same (and confusingly calling all three 'business model innovations') is wrong. This is a distinction that the literature has failed to make, and the result has been academic studies that are supposedly studying the same phenomenon when in fact they are studying apples with oranges. For the purposes of this Element, we will consider as BMI only those innovations that are either *new to the world* or *new to the industry*. In this regard, we differ from other researchers who consider *new-to-the-firm* business models as BMI (e.g. Amit and Zott, 2021). We disagree with this position because a business model that is new to the firm but not new to its industry or new to the world is simply a *change* of BM (and not an innovation in BM).

New-to-the-industry or new-to-the-world BMIs differ in their radicality – some will be more radical than others. This will be important in certain circumstances, but it will not affect the issues we tackle in this Element because what we are really interested in are innovations that introduce a way of competing that is *new to the industry of the established firm*. Their degree of radicality may make the challenge bigger but it doesn't change the challenge or add to it. They are new to the industry of the established firm, and that is all that matters for the purposes of this Element.

It is important to note that business model innovators do not discover new products or services – they simply redefine what an *existing* product or service is and how it is provided to the customer. For example, Amazon did not discover 'bookselling' – it redefined what the service is all about, what the customer gets out of it and how the service is provided to the customer. In addition, it is worth emphasizing that to qualify as an innovation, the new business model must enlarge the existing economic pie – either by attracting new customers into the market or by encouraging existing customers to consume more. This implies that a BMI is much more than the discovery of a radical new strategy or BM on the part of a firm – and that is why our definition of BMI excludes new-to-the-firm business models. For example, IBM's change of strategy in the early 1990s, radical as it may have been, is not a BMI. Similarly, Microsoft's 2014 adoption of a subscription model for its Office suite of applications – radical and beneficial as it might have been for Microsoft – is not a BMI. On the other hand, companies such as Amazon, Charles Schwab, Dell, IKEA, Uber, Airbnb and Southwest are considered business model innovators because they introduced business models that are new to their industries and in the process enlarged their markets by attracting new customers into them. Although there is some subjectivity in how one can measure 'new' or how novel a BMI is, it is possible to do so in a systematic way so that most people will agree that something is a BMI, at least ex post (e.g. Slywotzky, 1996).

Business Model Innovation Is Not a New Phenomenon

The business model concept is not new – its first use in the literature can be traced to Bellman et al. (1957), more than sixty years ago. Similarly, business model *innovation* is not a new or recent phenomenon. IKEA introduced a business model innovation in the 1950s, Nucor did so in the 1960s, Dell in the 1970s, Nespresso in the 1980s and EasyJet in the 1990s. Business model innovation has, therefore, been around for a long time. This raises the question: 'why the sudden popularity of business model innovation in the academic literature?' Over the past ten years, academic conferences have held special forums discussing the topic, journals have devoted special issues exploring the phenomenon and numerous academic papers have been published on it (Foss and Saebi, 2015; Massa, Tucci and Afuah, 2017). What can explain this surge in interest in BMI over the last few years?

The surge in interest can be traced to the fact that although the phenomenon of BMI is not new, there is something new about BMI today relative to fifty years ago. What is new is the number (and variety) of business models that are being introduced every year. Simply put, we have seen an exponential growth in the number of new business models being introduced in industry after industry. The major reason for this is digital technologies.

To appreciate why the digital revolution has led to the proliferation of new business models, consider a business model made up of say (for simplicity's sake), three interconnected activities, A, B and C. In this illustration, think of activity A as the choice of customers to target; activity B as the choice of products to offer them; and activity C as the choice of distribution channel. Again, for simplicity, assume that each activity has two possible levels or answers – for example, for activity A, we can choose to target segment X or segment Y; for activity B, we can offer product alpha or product beta; and for activity C, we can distribute our product though retailers or a direct sales force. Given this simplified model of only three activities and two levels for each activity, the maximum number of combinations of activities (that is, business models) that a firm can theoretically develop is *eight* ($2 \times 2 \times 2$).

What digital technologies have allowed for is the emergence of more options for each activity. For example, we can now segment the market into many more customer segments and offer many more products than the two we had before; or we could use the Internet to distribute the product in many more ways than the two we had before. For simplicity, assume that for each activity we now have three possible levels or answers – for example, for activity A, we can choose to target segment X or segment Y or segment Z; for activity B, we can offer product alpha or product beta or product gamma; and for activity C, we can distribute our product through retailers or a direct sales force or online. This means that the maximum number of combinations of activities (that is, business models) that a firm can theoretically develop is now twenty-seven ($3 \times 3 \times 3$). Needless to say, many of these possible combinations will not be internally consistent and can be readily dismissed. But equally, the number of viable possibilities for each activity that digital technologies have allowed us to come up with is probably much more than the three assumed so far. This implies that the possible combinations of activities (i.e. the number of business models) that we can come up with in any given industry is now large. Hence the proliferation of new business models that we have witnessed in the last twenty years. This explains the sudden popularity and interest in BMI.

2 Discovering New Business Models

New business models have the potential to create huge new markets on the periphery of established markets. The literature has already alerted us that this is the case and has further demonstrated that these new markets are composed of two types of customers: existing customers who desert the established competitors, and new customers that get attracted into the market for the first time (Christensen, 1997; Gilbert, 2003; Gilbert and Bower, 2002). In fact, as originally demonstrated by Christensen (1997), it is new customers that are initially attracted to the new business model and give it the early support that it needs to grow. It is only later that existing customers switch to the new offerings. It is in this sense that the new business model is an 'innovation' – it does not simply steal market share from established players, but it also *enlarges* the existing economic pie either by attracting new customers into the market or by encouraging existing customers to consume more. Thus, the innovation creates new value rather than simply transferring value from one firm to another.

As indicated before. the amount of new value created by the BMI will depend on a number of factors. For example, Markides, Larsen and Gary (2020) showed that the radicality of the BMI as well as the maturity of the industry, the number of firms engaging in BMI and the ease of imitation in the industry were all important factors that affected how much new value was created by a BMI.

This value-creating aspect of BMI has attracted the attention of academic researchers and, as a result, a large body of research has developed on the various ways companies can *discover* new business models (e.g. Amit and Zott, 2012 and 2021; Casadesus-Masanell and Ricart, 2010; Giesen et al., 2007; Girotra and Netessine, 2014; Johnson, Christensen and Kagermann, 2008; Markides, 1997; McGrath, 2010; Osterwalder and Pigneur, 2010; Sinfield et al., 2012; Slywotzky, 1996; Snihur and Zott, 2020; Zott and Amit, 2010). Valuable as this research and advice has been, it is still highly unlikely that it would be utilized by big, established firms to *discover* new business models.

This is not because the big firm lacks entrepreneurial spirit or suffers from cultural inertia, bureaucracy, big size, arrogance or old age – though all these factors are undoubtedly important killers of innovation in big firms (Amit and Zott, 2021; Chesbrough, 2010; Smith, Binns and Tushman, 2010). Rather, the fact is that BMI is a type of innovation that displays several characteristics that make it relatively unattractive to big, established companies.

Characteristics of Business Model Innovations

The first characteristic of BMI that makes it unattractive to established firms is the fact that the activities of the new business model are not only different but are often also incompatible with the activities of the business model that the established firm is already using to compete in its core business (Porter, 1996). This creates trade-offs for the established firm. For example, by selling their tickets online just like their low-cost competitors, established airline companies risk alienating their traditional distributors, the travel agents. Similarly, by moving into the selling of private label brands, fast-moving consumer goods (FMCGs) companies such as Unilever risk damaging their existing brands and diluting their organizations' strong cultures for innovation and differentiation.

Porter (1996) identified three main factors that give rise to such trade-offs. First, trade-offs arise from inconsistencies in a company's image or reputation. Second, they arise from the limits that a firm faces when it tries to coordinate and control incompatible sets of activities. Finally, trade-offs occur as a result of the particular set of activities that a company needs to compete successfully in its chosen strategic industry position. A unique strategic position requires a particular set of tailored activities – such as product configurations, distribution, value proposition, employee skills and management systems – that may be incompatible with the activities of alternative positions in the same industry. The existence of such trade-offs and conflicts means that a company that tries to compete in both positions simultaneously risks paying a huge straddling cost and degrading the value of its existing activities (Porter, 1996). The problem is obviously not insurmountable, but its very presence makes BMI a much more difficult proposition for established firms than for start-up firms.

The experience of Auto Trader Group plc – the United Kingdom's number one online marketplace for car buyers – is a classic example of the difficulties that an established player might face when it tries to adopt a BMI whose activities are incompatible with the activities of its existing business model. The company started life in 1977 as a print magazine featuring classified advertisements. The magazine was published weekly in twelve regional editions. The company was quick to recognize the potential of the internet and set up a separate unit called Autotrader Online to build an online business in 1996. It quickly became apparent that by going directly to the end consumer, the online unit was undermining the established distributors of the print side of the business, the car dealers. For example, the unit would promote products and features – such as reviews of dealers on the website – that consumers liked but dealers hated. Another example of the antagonism with the dealers surfaced during the 2008–9 recession. This was a period of economic hardship for the car dealers, but despite the difficult economic conditions, Auto Trader proceeded to implement a 30 per cent price increase, inflicting more pain on dealers. The relationship got so bad that the dealers organized themselves into a lobby to boycott advertising on the company's website. Even worse, the ten biggest dealers in the United Kingdom got together and set up their own website to compete with Auto Trader directly. The problems were eventually managed once a new CEO – Trevor Mather – was hired in 2013, but the fact that such problems surfaced to begin with and took more than seventeen years (1996–2013) to be sorted out indicates the magnitude of the problem that BMI presents to established firms.

The second characteristic that makes BMI unattractive to established firms is that BMI creates new markets that 'conflict with' and undermine the core business. They do so in two ways. First, the new market created by BMI requires investments to grow. These investments have to be financed somehow, and the resources almost invariably have to come at the expense of the core market. Second, it is often the case that the new market created by BMI grows by cannibalizing the core market. For example, (part of) the growth of the Nespresso market came at the expense of Nestlé's Nescafé brand. Similarly, the growth of the streaming business at SKY in the United Kingdom came at the expense of its much more profitable pay TV business. The fact that BMI creates markets that disrupt the core business makes BMI even more unattractive to the managers of the core business. As argued by Gilbert (2003), the managers of the core business end up seeing and treating BMI more as a threat than as an opportunity.

Again, the experience of Auto Trader highlights the severity of the problem. When the separate unit, Autotrader Online, was created in 1996, it was given full autonomy from the parent to grow the digital business. The original team of twenty were all new recruits from outside the core business, often described by core managers as 'young and arrogant'. They were given key performance indicators that were totally different from those used in the print business and they embarked on building the online business with a start-up mentality, avoiding any contact with the parent. Print circulation at the time was around 350,000 copies a week. Over time, the online business grew while the print business shrank. As one senior executive put it: 'the budget of the print side of the business got reduced every day; the attention it received got reduced every day; its headcount got reduced every day'. It did not take long for the magazine side to begin treating the unit as 'the enemy' and dysfunctional behaviours surfaced. As one senior executive commented: '*we transitioned our revenues online but not our culture and values*'. The antagonism between the print and digital sides of the business got so bad that the company had to change its top management team and change its original strategy to avoid bankruptcy. The story had a happy ending, but it again highlights the enormous challenge that BMI can present to a company that already has a core business to protect.

Certain types of business model innovations – but not all – display another characteristic that make them even more challenging for established firms.

Specifically, business model innovations such as the no-frills, point-to-point BMI introduced in the airline industry by companies such as Southwest and easyJet and the online brokerage BMI introduced by Charles Schwab in the mid-1990s follow closely the process of disruption first identified by Christensen (1997) in his examination of disruptive technologies (not BMI). These types of BMIs introduce products and services that – at least initially – are of little interest to the customers of the established companies. For example, whereas traditional brokers sold their services on the basis of their research and advice to customers, online brokers grew on the back of a different value proposition, namely price and speed of execution. Similarly, whereas traditional airline companies sold their product on the basis of frequency of flights, range of destinations and quality of service on board, low-cost, point-to-point operators emphasized price. Not only do new business models offer different performance attributes from the ones that mainstream customers historically value, but they also perform far worse – at least initially – along one or two dimensions that are particularly important to the mainstream customers (Christensen, 1997).

All this implies that the mainstream customers will not be interested in what the new business model is offering – at least initially (Christensen, 1997). Of course, the innovators who introduced the new business model will continue to invest in it and will, over time, improve it. It may eventually reach a point when its offerings become 'good enough' for the mainstream customers, at which point they will also start migrating to it (Christensen, 1997; Gilbert, 2003). This is what leads to the cannibalization of the core market. But this is a process that takes several years to play out and there is no certainty that the offerings of the new business model will ever improve enough to become 'good enough' for mainstream customers. What is certain is that at its inception, the new business model delivers something that is not good enough for the customers of the established firm and it is debatable whether it will do so in the future. This does not create the right incentives for the established firm to actively invest in developing new business models. Why invest in something that its customers do not want and may never want in the future?

It is important to emphasize that *not* all business model innovations display this particular characteristic, and we should not confuse disruptive BMI with Christensen's theory of disruptive innovation. Even casual examination of the business model innovations introduced by companies such as Netflix or Spotify or Perlego should make it abundantly clear that not all new business models follow the process of disruption described by Christensen (1997). All three of the previously mentioned BMIs started life by offering services that were immediately attractive to the mainstream customers rather than to a different customer. And all three offered services that went beyond just low price. So, there is no question that there are BMIs that do not display the last characteristic discussed earlier and we should not make the mistake of seeing BMI as just a repetition of Christensen's disruption process. But certain BMIs display this characteristic, something that makes them even more of a challenge for established firms.

Over and above the three characteristics described so far, we can list many more reasons why BMI is much less attractive as an investment for established companies than for start-up firms. For example, the markets created by BMI start out as small and insignificant compared to the main markets that the established firms are already operating in. As a result, it is difficult to generate entrepreneurial passion inside the big firm for these markets (Newman et al., 2021). Similarly, the new markets take time to grow and become profitable enough for the established firm. As a result, they run into the impatient capital problem that all publicly traded companies face (Laverty, 1996). But the three characteristics mentioned earlier are the primary reasons why big, established firms are unlikely to follow academic advice to 'innovate' and discover new business models – something that is supported by the fact that the majority of new business models, especially new-to-the world and new-to-the-industry ones, are introduced by start-up firms rather than established ones.

Discovering versus Scaling Up Business Models

The observation that the big, established firms are less likely than start-up firms to pioneer new business models should not be a source of concern. As originally pointed out by Schumpeter (1942), successful innovation is essentially a coupling process that requires the linking of two distinct activities: the discovery of a new product or service idea and its initial testing in the market that, if successful, creates a new market niche; and the transformation of the idea from a little niche into a mass market. Both activities are, obviously, important and necessary for successful innovation, but *there is no need for the same firm to do both*. In fact, it is often the case that the firm that comes up with a new radical idea – the pioneer – is not the one that creates a mass market out of that idea – the consolidator or scaler up (Markides and Geroski, 2005; Schnaars, 1994; Tellis and Golder, 2001; Watts, 2001). Everybody derides Xerox for discovering numerous products and technologies at its PARC research center and then failing to bring them to market. The truth of the matter is that this happens more often than we think.

More specifically, the evidence shows that it is usually small start-up firms that discover or pioneer radical innovations but it is usually big firms that scale up these discoveries. For example, consider the research findings reported by Schnaars (1994). Of the twenty-eight cases of radical product innovations that he examined, twenty-four of them were pioneered by small firms and only four by large firms. However, the majority of these discoveries (twenty-three out of twenty-eight) were taken up and subsequently scaled up into big mass markets by a big firm. He further found that there were only five cases where a small firm did the scaling up and there were no cases of a large firm pioneering and then being replaced by a small firm in scaling up the discovery. It appears that big, established firms have the skills and competences that allow them to excel in what is really the key in conquering new markets: taking an early market out of the hands of the pioneers and scaling it up into a mass market.

This is all good news for big, established firms. It implies that they could 'subcontract' the discovery of new business models to start-up firms so as to focus their attention on what they do best: scaling up new BMIs. *How* exactly to do this is the subject of another section in this Element. However, before moving from this point, it is worth emphasizing how counterintuitive such a proposition might appear to academics who have been proposing a host of revolutionary ideas on how to make big, established firms more innovative.

For example, Hamel (1996, 1999 and 2000) has proposed ideas such as making the strategy process democratic and bringing Silicon Valley inside the organization as ingredients to radical innovation. Similarly, Markides (1997, 1998) has argued that corporations could learn from the success of the capitalist system by importing into their organizations those features of capitalism (such as decentralized allocation of resources, multiple sources of financing and constant experimentation) that promote innovation. And Christensen et al. (2002) as well as Burgelman and Sayles (1986) have advocated the creation of separate units or divisions within an established organization where new disruptive growth businesses could be nurtured. These are all excellent ideas – but all of them aim to make the big firm better at 'creation' and discovery. When it comes to BMI, none of them will be particularly useful to the big, established firms. What prevents them from *discovering* new business models is not lack of creativity. Rather, it is organizational realities and the underlying incentives in the system.

When Will Big Firms Engage in Business Model Innovation?

Unquestionably, the characteristics of business model innovations are such that most established firms – especially successful ones – will find BMI an unattractive investment to undertake. There are, however, circumstances that create the right incentives for big, established firms to take the initiative in undertaking BMI (Markides, 2008).

The first is when the established firm is using a business model that is failing. The firm will then search to discover a new business model. It may not necessarily be the case that the new business model adopted will be new to the world or new to the industry, but in its search for a new winning strategy and business model, the firm may actually stumble upon a new business model that turns out to be a new-to-the-world one.

A second situation where the incentives will be in place for a big firm to undertake BMI is in entering a new market. One of the most robust findings from academic studies on new market entry is that most new entrants fail. For example, several studies of market entry in the United States, Canada and the United Kingdom have reported that about 5–10 per cent of new entrants disappear within a year of entry, 20–30 per cent disappear within two years and some 50 per cent disappear within five years of entry (Geroski, 1991). A second robust finding in this literature is that the probability of success in attacking established competitors through market entry is increased if the entrant adopts an innovative strategy, one that avoids imitation and instead disrupts the established players (Markides, 1997). As proposed by Porter (1985): 'The cardinal rule in offensive strategy is not to attack head-on with an imitative strategy, regardless of the challenger's resources or staying power.' Adopting such a strategy does not guarantee success but it improves the odds of success for the entrants. This implies that if an established company is contemplating entering a new market, it knows that it can increase its probability of success by adopting an innovative business model, one that is substantially different from the business models of the incumbents in the market it is about to enter. This might be enough of an incentive to engage in BMI.

The necessary incentives to develop a game-changing business model are also in place when established firms attempt to scale up a newly created market. As demonstrated by Markides and Geroski (2005), the early pioneers that create and colonize a new market do so by emphasizing the technical attributes and functionality of new products and services. In the process, they create the first market niche. However, for this niche to scale up, the basis of competition needs to shift from technical performance to other product attributes such as price and quality. After all, this is what the mass market demands. For this to happen, different firms – usually big, established firms – need to move into the market, take over the innovations of the early pioneers and scale them up by utilizing a new business model – one appropriate for the mass market. Once again, the big firm has the right incentives to engage in BMI in such a situation.

Although there are always circumstances under which big, established firms will invest in the discovery of a BMI, this should not take away from the key point in this section – that big, established firms are unlikely to be the ones to pioneer new business models. This is not a reflection of their lack of creativity or absence of entrepreneurial passion. It is, instead, a reflection of the characteristics of BMI that make it a less attractive investment for established firms than for start-up firms, in the majority of cases.

3 Responding to Business Model Innovation

New business models tend to be disruptive to the existing business models of the established firm (Christensen, 1997; Gilbert, 2003; Markides, 2008). As already mentioned, not only do new business models create markets that often cannibalize the core markets of the established firms, but they also employ value-chain activities that are different from, and incompatible with the activities of the established business model (Porter, 1996). For example, the new business model may utilize a new distribution method that will undermine and alienate the distributors in the core business; or it may promote brands that will dilute the value of the established brands. Given these characteristics, we have argued that established firms will have fewer incentives than start-up firms to *discover* or introduce new business models – an assertion supported by the evidence that the majority of new-to-the-world business models are introduced by start-up firms. These same characteristics also make it difficult for established firms to *respond* to the arrival of a BMI in their industries – and this may explain the poor track record of established firms in responding to BMI (Markides, 2008).

When it comes to the topic of responding to BMI, the existing literature has already explored a number of issues, including the response options available to established firms, the conditions that influence when to do what and the strategies that improve the probability of success of each response option (e.g. Charitou, 2001; Charitou and Markides, 2003; Cooper and Smith, 1992; Gilbert and Bower, 2002; Govindarajan and Trimble, 2005; Harren, Knyphausen-Aufseb and Markides, 2022; Khanagha et al., 2013; Markides and Charitou, 2004; Markides and Oyon, 2010; Sohl and Vroom, 2017; Visnjic, Wiengarten and Neely, 2016). A lot of this literature has focused on offering practical advice to managers on how to respond to BMI successfully. From an academic perspective, there are three main issues that have been the subject of disagreements and debate and deserve further analysis. These are as follows:

- is the process of disruption unstoppable and destined to play itself out no matter how much time it takes? If that is the case, then a logical implication is that the only viable response option for an established firm is to get on the bandwagon and adopt the new ways of competing.
- If the established firm chooses to *not* adopt a disruptive BMI, does that mean it is ignoring the BMI? If it chooses to continue with its existing BM, does that imply inaction on its part or can it continue to follow its existing BM and respond to the arrival of a disruptive BMI at the same time?
- If the established firm chooses to adopt the disruptive BMI, should it do so in a separate unit? Is separation the only way to succeed in competing with two different and disruptive business models simultaneously?

Is Disruption an Unstoppable Process?

In his early work on disruptive innovation, Christensen (1997) explored primarily examples of technological innovations and demonstrated how new technologies came to surpass seemingly superior technologies in the market. It was only in his later work (Christensen and Raynor, 2003) that the 'theory' of disruptive innovation was extended to explain not only technological innovations but also product and business model innovations. For example, Christensen and Raynor (2003) labelled as disruptive innovations such disparate things as discount department stores, online businesses such as bookselling, education, brokerage and travel agents and cheap, mass-market products such as power tools, copiers and motorcycles. Although all these innovations are 'disruptive' to established firms, treating them as one and the same phenomenon is a mistake. A disruptive business model innovation is not the same thing as a disruptive technological innovation, and mixing up the two has led to confusion and the emergence of several mistaken beliefs and misconceptions (King and Baatartogtokh, 2015).

One of the misconceptions to emerge is that disruptive innovation is an unstoppable process that will inevitably lead to the destruction of the status quo. This belief arose because it was probably true in the early work of Christensen that examined technological innovation. For example, the 14-inch disk drive – the main example in Christensen's early work – was destroyed by the 8-inch drive which, in turn, was destroyed by the 5.25-inch disk drive which, in turn, was destroyed by the 3.5-inch drive. In all, of the seventeen firms populating the hard disk drive industry in 1976, none except IBM's disk drive operation survived until 1996 (Christensen, 1997). Similar – but not as dramatic stories – could be told about the undermining of the integrated steel mills by mini-mills and the replacement of mainframe computers by personal computers. It is this evidence on the effect of disruptive *technological* innovations that led to the belief that disruptive innovation is an unstoppable process. For example, Christensen and Raynor (2003: 69) made the argument that 'disruption is a process and not an event . . . it might take decades for the forces to work their way through an industry but [they] are always at work'. Similarly, Danneels (2004: 247) summarized the existing theory of disruptive innovation by pointing out that 'disruptive technologies tend to be associated with the replacement of incumbents by entrants'.

It was at this point that Christensen broadened the concept of 'disruptive innovation' to include not only technological but also business model innovations. By including business models under the umbrella of 'disruptive innovation', it was an easy leap of logic to then assume that disruptive business models will also grow to dominate in their markets and in the process, destroy the existing business models. However, this is a mistake. We know this is a mistake because all available evidence shows that new markets created by BMI tend to grow to a certain per cent of the total market but rarely conquer the whole market. Nor do the new business models end up being the only way to compete in a given industry. For example, the no-frills point-to-point business model in the airline industry grew quickly to capture one-third of the market in Europe and the United States by 2000 but did not succeed in growing bigger than that. Similarly, internet banking may be the dominant way for most consumers to do their banking business these days, but it is hardly the only way.

Not only do we have evidence that disruptive business models rarely grow to completely dominate a market, but we also have a lot of research that explores the factors that determine how well the new business models will do in a market (Charitou, 2001; Chen and Miller, 1994; Chen, Smith and Grimm, 1992; Dutton and Jackson, 1987; Smith et al., 1991). Interestingly – and especially relevant for the discussion to follow this section – *one* of these factors is whether and how the established players respond to the BMI (Charitou, 2001; Markides, 2013). It has been shown, for example, that established firms can slow the growth of the markets created by BMI by investing to improve their own offerings and business models and in the process change consumers' perceptions of what is 'good enough' for them. The case of Gillette and its response to low-cost, disposable razors is a case in point. After seeing a third of the razor market being won over by Bic (in less than ten years), Gillette set about to change people's perceptions on what to expect from their razor. Through a series of innovative product introductions (such as the Sensor, the Mach 3 and the Fusion), Gillette redefined what 'performance' meant in this market. They also innovated in the disposable space – for example, in 1994 they introduced the Custom Plus line that was a disposable with a lubricating strip. By successfully raising the bar in this market, Gillette managed to convince consumers that they should expect more from their razors and that Bic was not really 'good enough' for them. In the process, they succeeded in maintaining their leadership position in refillables while capturing a 45 per cent market share in disposables.

Thus, whether the disruptive business models will grow to dominate a market or not will depend on several factors, one of which is whether and how the established players respond to these new business models. The likelihood and aggressiveness of the response by the established firms is, in turn, determined by several other factors (e.g. Atkinson, 1964; Chen, Smith and Grimm, 1992; Dutton and Jackson, 1987; House, 1971; Kiesler and Sproull, 1982; MacMillan, McCaffery and Van Wijk, 1985; Porter, 1980, 1985; Vroom, 1964). These factors have been grouped into three broad categories (Charitou, 2001): awareness, motivation and ability. The more *aware* incumbents are of a disruptive innovation and the more *motivated* and *able* they are to respond to it, the more aggressively they will be in responding to it. Therefore, any factor that influences the firm's awareness of the disruption or its motivation and ability to respond to it will influence how aggressively the firm responds.

Of the many factors that influence these three variables, two stand out (Charitou, 2001): degree of conflicts between the disruptor's business model and the incumbent's business model; and the magnitude of threat that the disruptive BMI poses to the incumbent's main business. The first variable – the degree of conflicts between the two business models – influences the firm's *ability* to respond: the higher the conflicts, the lower the ability to respond. The second variable – the magnitude of threat posed by the BMI – influences the firm's *motivation* to respond: the more threatening the disruption, the more motivated the incumbent to respond.

Of course, just because incumbents respond aggressively to a disruptive innovation does not necessarily mean that their efforts will be successful. In fact, the evidence shows that the attitudes and mindsets that incumbents bring into the battle are key to success (Gilbert, 2003). Specifically, we know that incumbents that look at the disruptive innovation as a threat to their business are likely to fail in their response. Those that are more likely to succeed are those that approach the disruption as both a threat and an opportunity. This allows them to respond with the appropriate level of urgency while at the same time maintaining a long-enough perspective to make the necessary investments.

In summary, then, we can see that whether BMI innovators succeed in capturing the established market depends a lot on how the incumbents respond. This, in turn, depends on too many factors to even begin listing here. But we can at least start to get a better idea on whether established firms will respond aggressively enough or whether they will have much success with their responses by thinking through the following questions:

- How threatening is the disruption to the incumbent's main business?
- How conflicting is the disruption to the incumbent's business model?
- How are the incumbents viewing the disruption?

Answering these questions will not give us a definite answer. But it will allow us to assess the probability that the incumbents will be successful in stopping disruptive innovations from destroying their markets.

Respond Does Not Mean Adopt

The mistaken belief that all disruptive innovations will eventually destroy and replace the status quo has led to an unfortunate misunderstanding in the BMI literature. This is the misunderstanding that 'responding' to a disruptive business model is equivalent to 'adopting' it in some way, something that will inevitably lead to the problems associated with competing in two strategic positions simultaneously – such as degrading the value of the firm's existing value-chain activities (Porter, 1996). For example, Amit and Zott (2021: 112) suggest that 'for the disrupted firm, failure to adopt the business model can entail serious negative performance consequences'. It is easy to see why this (mistaken) belief arose: if disruptive innovations are destined to conquer the market and destroy the status quo, then it follows that established firms have only one possible response option: adopt them. Failing to do so will lead to the demise of the incumbents, just like in the hard disk drive industry where all but one of the industry incumbents failed to adopt the new technologies and eventually exited the market.

We now see that in the case of BMI, this is a wrong belief to have. If we accept the premise that the BMI is not necessarily superior to the established firm's BM and that it is not destined to capture the whole market, the obvious implication that emerges is that it is not necessarily an optimal strategy for an established firm to abandon its existing BM in favour of the new one or to even adopt the BMI next to its existing BM. Other response options might exist, including deciding to focus on the existing business model or attempting to undermine the BMI through the strategy of 'disrupt-the-disruptor' (Markides, 2008; 2021). The decision should be based on a careful cost-benefit analysis and would depend on firm-specific circumstances as well as the nature of the innovation.

This might seem like an obvious argument to make, but it has been confused with inaction on the part of the firm. For example, Christensen (2006) objected to the idea that focusing on the existing BM might be a better investment than adopting the BMI by arguing: 'I had simply assumed that the objective function of management should be to maximize shareholder value. If survival is instead the objective function, then quite possibly inaction is a good course of action.' This confuses the strategy of focusing on one's existing business model with inaction and sees 'focusing' as synonymous with 'ignoring the BMI'. This is obviously a misconception, and the empirical evidence clearly shows that there are several ways in which the established firm can use the focus strategy to respond successfully to a disruptive BMI.

Focus Does Not Mean Ignore: The Case of Low-Cost Business Model Innovation

To appreciate the options available to an established firm on how to respond through the focus strategy, consider just one type of business model innovations that are possible: the ones that enter a new market as Christensen (1997) described through a low-cost strategy, targeting a different type of customer from the mainstream customer. As already discussed, this is not the only type of BMI available and the process through which this type of innovation enters the market is not the only way to attack a market. However, we will use this type of BMI as an example to make the case that focusing on the established business model is not synonymous with inaction.

As described by Christensen (1997), this type of disruptive business model makes inroads in the markets of the established firm through a predictable process: it starts out by being inferior in some performance attributes (usually functionality or quality) of the established BM but superior to it in something else (usually in cost, reflected in a lower price). This implies that when it starts out, mainstream customers will ignore the BMI, but other customers (different from the customers of the established firm) will be attracted to it because of its low price. Over time, the BMI will grow to become 'good enough' in perform-ance *while at the same time* remaining superior in price. This will allow it to attract the established customers as well, something that leads to the cannibal-ization of the core market of the established firm. It is important to appreciate that it is not enough for the BMI to be just 'good enough' in performance or to be just cheaper. It must be 'good enough' in performance *and* superior in price.

The key point here is that there is a dynamic element to the process of disruption. It is not how a BMI starts out that makes it disruptive. Rather, it is how it develops over time and how incumbents respond to it that makes it disruptive. This has the important implication that *you cannot tell ex ante whether a BMI will be disruptive or not* (Danneels, 2004). You can only tell after the fact. All you can do at the start of the disruption process is to assess the chances (or probability or *potential*) of a BMI evolving to become disruptive. And to do that, two questions need to be answered:

- Will the innovators *continue* to have a (significant) price advantage over the established firms?
- Will they succeed in *closing* the performance gap so that mainstream cus-tomers come to see their products or services as 'good enough'?

These two questions should immediately alert us to two key strategy options available to an established firm that is considering responding to a BMI by focusing on its existing BMI – the first is to attempt to improve its own business model so that the BMI no longer has a cost advantage; the second is to try to improve its own business model so that the BMI is not successful in convincing established customers that it is 'good enough' for them in performance.

The first way that established firms can improve their BM is by cutting their costs so that the BMI cannot claim to be superior to them on this dimension. Whether they will succeed in doing this depends on the *source* of the cost advantage that the disruptors enjoy. If the source of the cost advantage is low labour costs or a re-engineered product that requires fewer or cheaper components, the incumbents can find ways to neutralize these advantages. For example, if the source of the cost advantage is low labour costs, incumbents could simply transfer their manufacturing processes to lower-cost countries. If it is a re-engineered product, incumbents could undertake a similar re-engineering process with their own products. To see this, consider the case of the Swiss watch industry when it came under attack from cheap Japanese watches in the 1970s.

In the early 1960s, the Swiss dominated the global watch industry. This dominance all but evaporated in the 1970s when companies such as Seiko (from Japan) and Timex (from the United States) introduced cheap watches that used quartz technology and provided added functionality and features (such as the alarm function, date indication etc.). Swiss share of global world production declined from 48 per cent in 1965 to 15 per cent by 1980. In response, the Swiss (SMH) introduced the Swatch. Not only did the new watch introduce style as a competitive dimension but more importantly, it was sold at a price that was *close enough* to the average Seiko price. The Swatch was not cheaper than Seiko, but the tremendous price advantage that Seiko enjoyed was cut to a few dollars. Since its launch in 1983, Swatch has become one of the world's most popular timepieces with millions being sold all over the world every year.

How did the Swiss manage to cut the price of the Swatch to such low levels without moving manufacturing offshore? They achieved this by eliminating many of the product attributes that they thought were unnecessary (thus cutting costs) while enhancing certain other product features like style and design (thus building differentiation). They also found ways to cut other costs (in manufacturing and in materials used) and to build differentiation in other ways (for example, through the Swatch Club). The end result was a watch that all but eliminated the disruptors' price advantage (while offering a new differentiation benefit – style – as well). As a result, the Swiss succeeded in regaining most of their lost market share.

A cost advantage is very difficult to sustain, especially if the incumbents go about the business of cutting their costs in an aggressive and committed way. For example, Bic had an initial cost advantage over Gillette. Yet, Gillette succeeded in producing its own line of cheap, disposable razors that thwarted Bic's onslaught. Similarly, generic drugs use low price to attack branded drugs that come off patent. But there is no secret to their low-cost strategy and there's little that can prevent big pharmaceutical companies from doing the same. Novartis, GSK, Merck and Sanofi-Aventis are all examples of incumbents doing very well in producing and selling generic drugs. A similar pattern can be seen in a number of industries that were attacked by low-cost disruptors (such as the banking industry, the supermarket industry and the cosmetics industry), a fact that reinforces the point that a cost advantage is difficult to sustain for long.

The second way that established firms can improve their BM is by improving its performance to such an extent that the established customers stop considering the BMI to be 'good enough' in performance. There are two major ways to do this. The first is by focusing on the BMI's *existing value proposition* (such as performance) and raising that to higher levels. Doing so will keep raising the bar on what is good enough and make life more difficult for the disruptors. Gillette is an example of a company that did this in its response to disposable razors. A second way is to shift the basis of competition altogether, away from what the disruptors are trying to catch up with (i.e. performance) to another benefit. For example, SMH was able to shift customer attention away from performance to style and design, an area where the disruptor (Seiko) was not even considering.

The two strategies outlined here are not the only ones that the established firm can utilize to execute a focus strategy. Other strategies are possible and have been identified in the literature (Markides, 2021). For example, the established firm can identify weaknesses in the disruptor's BM and then adjust its own BM so as to exploit these weaknesses – as Walmart did in developing its online strategy to respond to Amazon. Additionally, the established firm could identify elements of the BMI that can be imported into its own BM so as to improve it – as British Airways did in developing its focus strategy to respond to the EasyJet business model. The established firm can also eliminate activities in its own BM that the BMI has made unnecessary, and so improve its BM in the process – as many companies are doing by distributing or selling directly to their customers, bypassing intermediaries. The established firm may even identify entirely new things to add to its own BM so as to make it even more competitive relative to the BMI – as John Deere has done in using big data to revolutionize the services it is offering to farmers. The options available to established firms seem to be limitless.

In summary, therefore, the key takeaways from this discussion are (i) responding to a disruptive BMI does not mean adopting the BMI – other response options are possible; (ii) one possible response option for the established firm is to focus on its existing business model; (iii) focusing on one's existing business model does not mean ignoring the BMI – it means thinking creatively about improving the existing BM so as to make it even more competitive relative to the BMI; and (iv) there are numerous ways through which the established firm can improve its existing business model. For example, it can reduce its costs to make it more price-competitive with the BMI; it can innovate in its BM so as to convince its customers that the BMI is not good enough relative to its own 'new and improved' BM; it can change its own BM in ways that allow it to exploit weaknesses in the BMI; or it can 'import' into its own BM selected elements of the BMI so as to improve its own BM. In short, the established firm has a huge number of ways in which it can improve its own BM to make it even more competitive relative to the BMI.

Adopting the Business Model Innovation

An alternative to using one's own BM to respond to a BMI is to adopt the BMI next to the existing business model – either as part of the firm's migration process from the existing BM to the new one or as a permanent solution. This raises quite a few challenges for the established firm, including the challenge of managing two different and conflicting business models simultaneously. We will cover this topic in the next section.

4 Competing with Two Business Models

One response option available to the established firm is to adopt the BMI next to its existing BM. The question that immediately arises is how to compete with two different and conflicting business models in the same industry. This is one of the thorniest issues that has emerged in the BMI literature and one that has been explored only through (primarily) case study research. The need to study this issue through more rigorous empirical methods is obvious. As argued by Snihur and Tarziján (2018: 51), 'the challenges of managing multiple BMs have not been studied in the detail they deserve'.

As already mentioned, this is a challenging task because the new business model requires different and often incompatible value chain activities from the ones that the established company has in place for its traditional business model (Porter, 1980, 1996). The existence of such trade-offs and conflicts means that a company that tries to compete in both positions simultaneously risks paying a huge straddling cost and degrading the value of its existing activities (Porter, 1996). The task is obviously not impossible, but it is certainly difficult. This is the logic that led Michael Porter (1980) to propose more than forty years ago that a company could find itself 'stuck in the middle' if it tried to compete with both low-cost and differentiation strategies.

The main solution offered in the literature on how to manage two different and conflicting business models simultaneously is *spatial separation* – in other words, keep the two business models (and their underlying value chains) physically separate in two distinct organizations. This is the 'innovator's solution' that's primarily associated with Christensen's (1997) work on disruptive innovation, but other academics have advocated it as well (e.g. Bower and Christensen, 1995; Burgelman and Sayles, 1986; Cooper and Smith, 1992; Gilbert and Bower, 2002; Utterback, 1996). For example, in their study of technological innovations, Cooper and Smith (1992) found that '*in a number of cases where the new and traditional technologies were fundamentally different, decisions to use the established organization proved to be ill-advised*' (1992: 64). Similarly, Bower and Christensen (1995), who were the first to introduce this idea into the literature on *business model* innovations, proposed that '*To commercialize and develop the new technologies, managers must protect them from the processes and incentives that are geared to serving established customers. And the only way to protect them is to create organizations that are completely independent from the mainstream business*' (1995: 44–45).

Even Porter (1996) has come out in favour of this strategy. Despite arguing that most companies that attempt to compete with dual strategies will likely fail, he has also proposed that '*companies seeking growth through broadening within their industry can best contain the risks to strategy by creating stand-alone units, each with its own brand name and tailored activities'* (Porter, 1996: 77).

The rationale for this solution is quite straightforward. The presence of conflicts and trade-offs between the two business models means that the parent organization and its managers will often find that the new business model is growing at their expense. They will therefore have incentives to constrain it or even kill it (e.g. Christensen, 1997; Porter, 1996). Therefore, by keeping the two business models separate, you prevent the company's existing processes and culture from suffocating the new business model. The new unit can develop its own culture, processes and strategy without interference from the parent company. It can also manage its business as it sees fit without being suffocated by the managers of the established company who see cannibalization threats and channel conflicts at every turn.

Sensible as this argument might be, the separation solution is not without problems and risks. Perhaps the biggest cost of keeping the two businesses separate is failure to exploit synergies between the two. For example, Day et al. (2001: p. 21) have argued that *'the simple injunction to cordon off new businesses is too narrow. Although ventures do need space to develop, strict separation can prevent them from obtaining invaluable resources and rob their parents of the vitality they can generate.'* Similarly, Iansiti, McFarlan and Westerman (2003: p. 58) reported that *'spinoffs often enable faster action early on but they later have difficulty achieving true staying power in the market. Even worse, by launching a spinoff, a company often creates conditions that make future integration very difficult.'*

In recognition of the need to exploit the synergies between the two business models, the argument in favour of separation has now been revised to one that proposes the creation of separate units that are linked together by a number of integrating mechanisms. For example, O'Reilly and Tushman (2004) proposed that a truly ambidextrous organization is one where separate units are integrated into the existing management hierarchy of the firm by having a common general manager to supervise them all. Similarly, Ghoshal and Gratton (2003) argued in favour of creating incentives that encourage cooperation among the separate units; Gilbert (2003) proposed the creation of an active and credible integrator to help units cooperate; and Govindarajan and Trimble (2005) proposed systems and cultures that allow the parent and the separate unit to work together while maintaining their independence. Numerous other studies have studied other kinds of integrating mechanisms that successful companies have put in place, and the list is large (Govindarajan and Trimble, 2005).

The proposed solution for separating the two business models (with integrating mechanisms in place) has received widespread acceptance in the literature on business models despite undergoing little or no empirical testing. We certainly have anecdotal evidence of companies that adopted this solution successfully, such as Nestlé and Nespresso; BNP Paribas and Hello Bank; The Cooperative Bank and Smile Bank; National Australia Bank and Ubank; Rabobank and RaboDirect; ASB Bank Australia and BankDirect; Qantas and Jetstar; Lufthansa and Germanwings; Waitrose and Ocado; Royal & Sun Alliance and MORE TH>N; Medtronic and Nayamed. However, we also have lots of examples of companies that adopted this solution and failed. Examples include British Airways and GO; KLM and Buzz; United and Ted; Continental Airlines and Continental Lite; Delta and Song; Air New Zealand and Freedom Air; Lloyds TSB bank and Evolve; Santander and Cahoot; Banque d'Escompte and First-e; Safeway and GroceryWorks.com; Royal Ahold and Peapod; Barnes & Noble and Bn.com. Crucially, we have examples of companies that successfully adopted a different BM next to their existing BM without creating a separate unit. Examples include numerous banks that – unlike BNP Paribas or Rabobank – adopted internet banking next to their core business model; as well as supermarket companies – such as TESCO and Sainsbury – that adopted online distribution of groceries as part of their existing business model.

What this evidence suggests is that creating a separate unit to adopt a BMI is *not always* necessary and is certainly not sufficient for successfully competing with two business models at the same time. The first insight – that a separate unit is not always the way to go – is an idea that emerges from the available anecdotal evidence, but it's also one that the extant literature on ambidexterity clearly makes (Markides, 2013). The literature on ambidexterity is a good foundation to rely on for insights on the topic of managing dual business models because this literature has been exploring the challenge of managing dualities – such as exploration and exploitation, efficiency and flexibility, differentiation and low cost, integration and responsiveness, and so on (Gulati and Puranam, 2009). Since the management of two conflicting business models is but one of these dualities, it follows that this literature can be used to help us develop insights on how best to do so.

One of these insights to emerge from the ambidexterity literature is that the separation solution is not the only one available in managing two business models. Other strategies are possible including the strategy of *temporal* separation (Nickerson and Zenger, 2002; Puranam, Singh and Zollo, 2006; Siggelkow and Levinthal, 2003). The main idea behind this proposal is that the same unit or company can undertake two seemingly incompatible activities (such as exploitation and exploration) but at different times. For example, Siggelkow and Levinthal (2003) showed through simulations of adaptation on rugged landscape that there are advantages to organizational forms that are initially decentralized but eventually centralized.

Yet another possible strategy is structural modulation (Nickerson and Zenger, 2002). This strategy allows for elements of *formal* and *informal* organization to be combined in unique ways – under certain conditions, managers modulate between or among discrete structures to dynamically position the informal organization at levels that approximate optimum functionality. In a similar vein, Gulati and Puranam (2009) explored the interplay between formal and informal organization in shaping organizational outcomes. They argued that the locus of decision-making on how to allocate efforts towards each pole of the duality should rest with the employees rather than a central organization designer. Their proposition is that the formal and informal organization will enable and encourage individuals to make their own judgements about how to divide their time between conflicting demands.

These ideas can easily be placed under the umbrella of *contextual* ambidexterity originally proposed by Gibson and Birkinshaw (2004). Based on the argument that the organizational context determines how people behave, they proposed that the organization ought to design the appropriate context that would encourage and support each employee to achieve an appropriate level of balance between the conflicting demands on their time and attention. Thus, to manage two conflicting business models simultaneously, an organization needs to ask and answer the question: 'what *organizational context* do I need to put in place to allow my people to achieve an appropriate level of balance between the conflicting demands they are facing?' By 'organizational context' we mean the firm's culture, values, structures and processes and the underlying measurement and incentives in the system. This suggests that the existing literature has focused exclusively (and unnecessarily) on a structural solution to the challenge of competing with dual business models when it should be looking more broadly at *all* the elements that make up the organizational context of a firm. We will return to this point later when we explore what else is needed – beyond a separate unit – to manage dual business models simultaneously.

Overall, the first generalization that emerges on the challenge of competing with two different and conflicting business models is that creating a separate unit to house the BMI is not the only viable way to manage this challenge. The existing literature has focused exclusively on separation as the solution when in fact the empirical evidence and the related ambidexterity literature suggest that other solutions may be optimal.

In Need of Contingencies

The fact that several strategies could be used to manage two different and conflicting business models at the same time naturally raises the question: 'when is one strategy preferable to the other?' Answering this question will lead us to a contingency theory that would outline under what conditions the separation strategy is the optimal approach and under what conditions the temporal separation or contextual ambidexterity strategies will be the optimal ones.

Some work has been done in this direction. For example, Markides and Charitou (2004) proposed that two key factors influence the choice of organizational strategy: first, how serious the conflicts between the two business models are – because this determines whether a *separation* strategy would be especially beneficial or not; and second, how strategically related the new market is perceived to be to the existing business – because this determines how important the exploitation of *synergies* between the two will be. Depending on how big or serious these conflicts or synergies are, different organizational strategies may be appropriate. They specifically argued that separation will be the preferred strategy when the new market is not only strategically different from the existing business but also when the two business models faced serious trade-offs and conflicts. By contrast, the temporal separation scenario became preferable when the new market was strategically similar to the existing business, but the two business models faced serious conflicts. In such a case, it might be better to separate for a period of time and then slowly merge the two concepts so as to minimize the disruption from the conflicts.

Research by Harren, Knyphausen-Aufseb and Markides (2022) complemented these findings by suggesting a number of additional factors that would influence which organizational strategy would be optimal. In their research, they used simulation experiments to show that even though the separation strategy will be *on average* the optimal one, there are circumstances when spatial separation becomes preferable. Specifically, spatial separation was found to be the optimal strategy when (a) the external environment undergoes frequent or big changes; (b) visibility of interdependencies between the two business models is high; (c) decisions between the two units are aligned; and (d) the two business models are weakly linked.

These results are consistent with the argument that the choice of organizational strategy will be influenced by the presence of conflicts between the two business models as well as the presence of synergies between the established market and the market created by the BMI. The relative number and strength of these conflicts and synergies also will have an effect. But obviously these factors are not the only ones that affect the organizational choice, as evidenced by the results in Harren et. al. (2022). More work on this topic will be helpful. But the results so far suggest that one reason why many companies fail despite choosing the separation strategy may be because this particular strategy may have been inappropriate given the conditions they were facing.

Separation May Be Necessary But Not Sufficient

So far, we have argued that a possible reason why some companies succeed in competing with dual business models through a separate unit while others fail may be because the choice of the separate unit was the wrong one for their circumstances. But there could be another reason for the same finding. It could be that the separation strategy is necessary but not sufficient to lead to success.

The literature on *contextual* ambidexterity suggests several additional things that need to be put in place for the separation strategy to succeed, one of which is the *degree* of separation between the parent firm and the new unit that has been created to house the new business model. In the original formulation of the separate unit solution, the argument was made that the new unit ought to develop its own tailored value-chain activities, completely separate from those of the parent firm (Christensen, 1997; Gilbert, 2003; O'Reilly and Tushman, 2004; Porter, 1996). Not only should the unit have its own value-chain activities, but it should also be allowed to develop its own name, culture and values, structures and processes and its own measurement systems and incentives (Christensen and Raynor, 2003; Govindarajan and Trimble, 2005; Porter, 1996).

Although these ideas were put forward by some of the most prominent scholars in strategy such as Clay Christensen and Michael Porter, the literature on contextual ambidexterity suggests that this may not be the right approach. Contextual ambidexterity suggests that to manage two business models simultaneously, the firm needs to design an organizational context that would allow it to achieve a delicate balance – on the one hand, it has to create enough distance between the two business models so that they don't suffocate each other; on the other hand, it has to keep them close enough to each other so that they can exploit any synergies between them. Such a balance will never be achieved if the new business model is kept totally separate from the established one. It can only be achieved if the firm thinks creatively on what specific activities it needs to separate and what activities not to (Gulati and Garino, 2000).

This decision on the appropriate degree of separation must be made for a number of areas. Markides and Oyon (2010) have proposed five such areas:

(a) *Location*: Should the separate unit be located close to the parent firm or far away from it?
(b) *Name*: Should the separate unit adopt its parent's name or something close to its parent's name, as United did with its low-cost unit that was called Ted or as Nestlé did with its Nespresso unit; or should its name be totally different from its parent, such as BA did with its low-cost unit that was called GO or as HSBC Midlands did with its telephone banking unit that it called First Direct?

(c) *Equity*: Should the unit be a wholly owned subsidiary of the parent, or should the parent own only a certain percentage of the equity?

(d) *Value-chain activities*: Which value-chain activities should the unit develop on its own and which should it share with the parent? The usual answer is to allow the unit to develop its own dedicated customer-facing activities and share its back-office activities with the parent. This, however, may not be the appropriate solution for every firm, so this issue has to be considered on a case-by-case basis.

(e) *Organizational Environment*: Should the unit be allowed to develop its own culture, values, processes, incentives and people, or should any of these be shared with the parent? Again, the usual answer is to allow the unit to develop its own culture but unite the parent and the unit through the adoption of common shared values. This, however, may not be appropriate for every firm, so this is again something that needs to be considered on a case-by-case basis.

Obviously, there are no 'right' answers to these questions. The important point to note, however, is that contrary to what many academics have proposed, the separate unit does not need to have its own name, nor does it have to develop its own dedicated value-chain activities. We have numerous examples of companies that did not do this and still succeeded in competing with two different and conflicting business models at the same time. The trick is to find the firm-specific answers to these questions that allow the firm to achieve the delicate balance between providing the unit independence and still helping it with the skills, knowledge and competences of the parent company (Govindarajan and Trimble, 2005; Markides, 2008).

The firm needs to decide not only on the appropriate degree of separation between the parent and the separate unit but also on the appropriate degree of integration between the two. Earlier, we discussed the importance of putting integrating mechanisms in place to exploit any synergies between the parent and the unit. The underlying assumption was that all firms need the same level of exploitation of synergies. This is obviously a simplification. The potential for synergies varies by company depending on how strategically similar the two markets that the two business models are serving are. This means that the level of integration needed should vary by company as well. As a result, different companies must put in place different levels of integrating mechanisms. Rather than develop a generic list of integrating mechanisms, future research must explore what kind of integrating mechanisms work for what kind of firms.

Beyond Structural Solutions

Deciding what activities of the unit will be shared with the parent company and which ones will be specifically designed for the unit is one of the things that the established firm must do to increase the probability of success of managing dual business models through a separate unit. There are more.

As argued earlier, the literature on contextual ambidexterity proposes that an organization needs to ask and answer the question: 'what organizational context do I need to put in place to allow my people to achieve an appropriate level of balance between the conflicting demands they are facing?' If we define 'organizational context' as the firm's culture, values, structure, processes and incentives, then this question makes it abundantly clear that the existing literature has been looking at the issue of competing with dual business models in a very narrow way. Specifically, the existing literature has focused primarily on structural solutions to manage this dilemma when in fact we should be looking more broadly at *all* the elements that make up the organizational context. In this respect, the work of O'Reilly and Tushman (2011) that emphasized the importance of vision, strategic intent, values, incentives and leadership in achieving ambidexterity is a step in the right direction.

Some research has been undertaken to identify factors that will help the established firm succeed in its efforts to compete with dual business models through the use of a separate unit. For example, Gilbert (2003) proposed that the parent firm's attitudes and mindsets towards the disruptive BMI are an important ingredient for success. He argued that by approaching a disruptive BMI as a threat to the core business, established firms respond to it with a defensive attitude. As a result, their emphasis is to defend and protect their main market rather than exploit the new market that the disruptive BMI has created. This defensive attitude leads them to short-term oriented actions that compromise the viability of their chosen strategy. More often than not, their response ends in failure. Surprisingly, a similar fate awaits those firms that approach BMI as an opportunity. Doing so allows them to develop a thoughtful and long-term oriented strategy but fails to create the necessary urgency for action. Gilbert, therefore, proposed that looking at the BMI as either a threat or an opportunity will be a mistake. The correct way to approach it will be as both a threat and an opportunity.

A complementary finding has been reported by Markides (2015a). He found that the companies that were more likely to fail with their separate unit were those that approached the new market created by the BMI as a simple extension of their core market rather than as a totally new market. On the face of it, approaching the new market as an extension of the core market is the most natural thing to do. After all, what is the difference between the low end of the airline market and the established airline market? Aren't they simply two segments of the same market? Similarly, what is the difference between trad-itional banking and online banking? Are they not just 'banking' and would we be wrong to see them as belonging to the same market? Though it seems natural to see the new markets as extensions of the core market, Markides (2015a) reported that doing so will be a mistake. Those companies that followed this approach fell into the trap of believing that assets, mental models and strategies that worked well in their core market would also work well in the new market. As a result, they 'imported' the mental models and strategies of the core business into the new market, something that backfired on them. The companies that were more likely to succeed with their separate unit were those that looked at the new market created by the disruptive BMI as a fundamentally *different* market from their core market. As a result, they approached the new market like entrepreneurs and designed a strategy for it that was not constrained by the mental models of the core business.

Another factor that was found to be important was agility (Markides, 2015a). This is important because the decision on what to separate and what to keep integrated is always taken at a point in time. At that point, given the existing conditions, the organization chooses what it considers to be the appropriate balance between integration and separation. But over time, conditions change – for example, the conflicts between the two business models may become more or less acute; the synergies between the two businesses may grow or decrease; and learning on how to manage the unit next to the parent increases over time. This suggests that the appropriate balance between separation and integration changes over time (Nickerson and Zenger, 2002). For example, incentive systems that were appropriate early on in the life of the new unit may become counterproductive later on and have to be changed. This suggests that the organization needs to develop the agility to change its choices over time. Only those companies that adjust the relationship between the parent company and the new unit over time, as conditions change, can hope to manage the unit successfully.

Yet another variable that influenced success was the extent to which the separate unit was allowed to not just imitate the BMI but to change it in ways that suited its specific circumstances (Markides, 2015a). For example, as argued already, the creation of a separate unit is undertaken primarily to minimize the tensions and frictions between the managers of the core business and the managers of the new unit that inevitably arise because of the conflicts between the two BMs. However, it is important to appreciate that while helpful, separ-ation does not eliminate the conflicts. They are still there and they still need to be managed. One way to manage these conflicts is by allowing the separate unit to develop a business model that explicitly takes into consideration these conflicts. The same goes for other unique challenges that the new unit might face in its market. The point is that the new unit operates in a different market with its own challenges, so the more freedom it has to develop its own unique strategy, the better.

For example, Markides (2015a) found that established firms that allowed the separate unit to develop a strategy that was differentiated from the strategy of the disruptors who introduced the BMI were more successful than those companies that gave less autonomy to their unit to develop a differentiated strategy. For example, in 1993 Continental Airlines created a separate subsidiary called Continental Lite and set about to capture market share in the low-cost, no-frills, point-to-point airline market that Southwest had pioneered. Unfortunately for Continental, the strategy adopted by its Lite subsidiary was an almost replica of the Southwest strategy. As a result, it failed to make any inroads and Continental shut the unit down in 1994. European airline companies like BA (with its GO subsidiary) and KLM (with its Buzz subsidiary) had the exact same experience as Continental: they entered the new market using the same business model as the (European) disruptors – in this case easyJet and Ryanair – and ended up selling or shutting down their operations within a few years of entry.

Giving the unit the freedom and autonomy to develop a business model that takes into consideration its own unique circumstances may seem like an obvious thing to do, but it is actually the exact opposite of what the unit would naturally do. Imagine you are British Airways. You have created a separate unit called GO that sets about competing in the new low-cost market that EasyJet has created. What is the most natural thing for GO to do in this new market? Obviously to imitate the very successful business model of easyJet that created the market in the first place! You know that the easyJet business model is a winning BM, so why deviate from it? Yet, that would probably be the worst thing to do. As proposed earlier, the new unit will increase its chances of success by developing a differentiated business model that takes into consideration its own specific circumstances. This is sensible advice but obviously difficult to put into practice.

Reinventing the Wheel

Approaching the task of competing with dual business models with the right attitude and the right mindsets and allowing the unit to develop its own business model are only a few of the additional things that a firm must do, over and above creating a separate unit. There are many more things that can be done. However, before encouraging BMI researchers to embark on research projects to uncover what other things might be useful, it may be useful to stop for a minute and ponder whether doing so will be a waste of time in that we will be reinventing the wheel.

As argued by Markides (2015b), the growing literature on business models has so far had limited impact on research in strategy. The main reason for this is the fact that the intellectual territory of the business model construct overlaps significantly with that of strategy. Without acknowledging this overlap, academics doing research on business models run the risk of asking questions that have already been explored in the strategy literature. The question of what factors can help the established firm succeed in its efforts to compete with dual business models through the use of a separate unit is a case in point. Research in the fields of technological innovation, ambidexterity, the transnational organization, organization design and strategic innovation has already explored this issue but with a different focus. For example, the literature on the transnational organization (Bartlett and Ghoshal, 1989) has already explored how the multinational firm can manage different subsidiaries so as to achieve centralization and decentralization at the same time. The same can be said for the literature on strategic innovation (Govindarajan and Trimble, 2005) where the question explored was how to build tomorrow's businesses while simultaneously sustaining excellence in today's business. There's therefore a rich literature on this topic which has already uncovered quite a few ideas on what a firm needs to do in addition to creating a separate unit. Some of these ideas are presented in Table 2.

This suggests that before embarking on new research projects to answer this question, it is worthwhile to consider what other literatures have already discovered or would suggest as the important questions to focus on. This is a strategy that Markides (2013) put to good use by borrowing from the literature on ambidexterity to develop insights on how a firm can compete with two business models at the same time. More generally, research on business models can only become more impactful if we first identify explicitly what is different between the business model and strategy concepts and then focus our research questions on that difference (Markides, 2015b).

Variants to Separation

Two variants to the separate unit solution have been proposed in the literature that deserve special mention. The first is called 'phased integration' and was proposed by Khanagha et al. (2013) to describe how a European telecom company developed its cloud business model. This involved starting the new business model in a separate unit but slowly re-integrating it into the existing

Table 2 What else to do over and above creating a separate unit

- Employ a common general manager between the main and the new business (O'Reilly and Tushman, 2004).
- Allow different cultures to emerge but unite the two with a strong shared vision (O'Reilly and Tushman, 2004).
- Staff the new business model with ambidextrous individuals (Gibson and Birkinshaw, 2004).
- Legitimize diverse perspectives and capabilities (Bartlett and Ghoshal, 1989).
- Build strong shared values that unite the people in the two businesses (Bartlett and Ghoshal, 1989).
- Do everything to avoid a silo mentality (for example, transfer of people, common conferences, rituals) (Bartlett and Ghoshal, 1989).
- Fund it in stages (Gilbert and Bower, 2002).
- Cultivate outside perspective by hiring new people for the separate unit (Gilbert, 2003; Gilbert and Bower, 2002).
- Appoint an active and credible integrator (Gilbert and Bower, 2002).
- Emphasize 'soft' levers such as a string sense of direction, strong values, a feeling of 'we are in this together' (Ghoshal and Gratton, 2003).
- Develop incentives that encourage cooperation between the two (Ghoshal and Gratton, 2003).
- Hire outsiders to run the unit with a mixture of insiders (Govindarajan and Trimble, 2005).
- Integrate the activities that cannot be done well if they become independent (Christensen and Raynor, 2003).
- Allow the unit to borrow brand name, physical assets, expertise and useful processes (Govindarajan and Trimble, 2005).
- Give the unit enough power to fight in its own corner (Govindarajan and Trimble, 2005).
- Ensure adequate flow of information through transfer of people and the intranet (Day, Mang, Richter and Roberts, 2001).
- Insulate the unit but don't isolate it (Markides, 2008).
- Give the new unit operational autonomy but exercise strong central strategic control (Markides and Charitou, 2004).
- Give the unit autonomy but don't lose control (Markides and Charitou, 2004).
- Allow the unit to differentiate itself by adopting a few of its own value-chain activities but at the same time exploit synergies by ensuring that some value-chain activities are shared (Markides and Charitou, 2004).
- Evaluate the unit subjectively (Govindarajan and Trimble, 2005).

organization – an approach also followed by numerous other companies such as BMW, British Airways, Barnes and Noble, Charles Schwab and the Danish bank Lan & Spar. The second is called 'phased separation' and involved starting the new business model inside the existing organization and then spinning it off as a separate unit once it grew to a certain size (Markides and Charitou, 2004).

These approaches are interesting because they introduce a dynamic element to the challenge of creating a separate unit to compete with dual business models. They show that a solution that may be optimal at a point in time may not be optimal over time. In fact, simulation results by Harren et al. (2022) found the phased integration strategy to be the optimal *long-term* strategy in the majority of cases. By contrast, the separation strategy was optimal only in the short term. The reason for this is simple enough: in the separation strategy, the parent and the unit optimized their own performance with little consideration of how their own decisions were affecting the other unit. As a result, they often settled for *local* optima which were suboptimal from the firm perspective. Each business unit optimized its own performance and thereby missed the decisions that would increase the overall firm performance.

The same study also showed that a key factor for the phased integration strategy to succeed was deciding exactly when to reintegrate the unit into the parent organization. Simulation results suggested that reintegration must take place much earlier than normal when the interdependencies between the business models were complementary rather than substitutes, suggesting the presence of synergies; and in the absence of visibility of interdependencies between the two business models. Finally, the results suggested that continued separation of the two units would not be a good idea if the interdependencies between the two business models were not actively managed.

Overall, the question of how to compete with two different and conflicting business models in the same industry is one of the most interesting topics to have emerged in the BMI literature. A lot of progress has been made in answering this question, but many other issues remain unanswered. This would be fertile ground for additional research.

5 The Uniqueness of Business Model Innovation

There is no question that BMI has attracted a lot of attention over the last few years in both the academic and business literatures. Yet, there is also no question that the impact of the business model literature on thinking about strategy has been marginal at best. For example, in a survey of forty strategy academics, Markides (2015b) found that although they all agreed that the BM construct was theoretically different from that of strategy, only a small minority (12 per cent) felt that the BM literature has enriched the strategy field in significant ways.

There are many reasons for this perception, but Markides (2015b) proposed that a key one might be the fact that there is significant overlap between the intellectual territory of the business model construct with that of strategy. As a result, academics doing research on business models end up asking questions or doing research on topics that have already been explored in the strategy literature. As an example of this problem, he points to one of the main questions that has preoccupied academic researchers in the business model field, namely the process by which a new business model can be developed. Although this is undoubtedly an interesting question, the problem (at least from a theoretical point of view) is that there is no reason to expect that the process of developing a new *business model* is any different from the process of developing a new *strategy*. Both strategy and BM describe (in varying degrees of detail) how a firm operates in its market, and ideas on how to change or modify this way of operating in the market (that is, ideas on the process to develop a new BM or a new strategy) could come about via numerous routes, including analysis, trial and error, intuition, luck, questioning of existing mental models, analogical thinking, creative segmentation, exploring customer gaps and so on. The list of possible ways is huge – and is already available in the strategy literature. This begs the question: 'What would be the theoretical contribution of repeating this list in the business model literature?' Sure enough, the answers that business model researchers have developed in response to this question are exactly the same as those found in the strategy literature. No wonder critics of the BMI literature claim that 'there is nothing new here'.

If the problem is too much overlap between the intellectual territory of strategy and BM, then the solution for researchers interested in exploring issues that are unique to the business model construct is to identify theoretical areas of little or no overlap and use that as the platform to develop research questions that have not already been explored in strategy. To make progress, therefore, we must first identify this 'no-overlap' theoretical region and then develop and answer questions derived specifically from this theoretically unexplored territory. Two such areas, unique to the business model construct, stand out.

A System of Interrelationships

The most prominent feature of the business model construct is the fact that the (many) activities that make up a business model are interconnected. Much more important than deciding on what activities to undertake, a firm must find a way of combining them into *a system* that creates the requisite fit first between the activities themselves and second, between the whole system and the outside environment facing the company. Making sure that the activities fit together into a well-balanced system is much more critical and important than developing the individual activities. As Porter (1996: 70) argued: 'strategy is about *combining* activities'. This idea is not new. It is one of the founding principles of 'system dynamics' as developed by Jay W. Forrester at the Massachusetts Institute of Technology. A powerful managerial exposition of system dynamics and systems thinking principles can be found in Senge (1990).

The importance of conceptualizing the company as a combination of interdependent activities cannot be overemphasized. In this perspective, a firm is a complex system of interrelated and interdependent activities, each affecting each other: decisions and actions in one part of the business affect other parts, directly or indirectly. Thus, unless managers take a holistic, big-picture approach in designing their company's activities, their efforts will backfire. Even if each individual activity is optimally crafted, the whole may still suffer unless their interdependencies are properly taken into consideration. The risk is that trying to achieve several local optima in the system will almost always undermine the global optimum.

Again, this is not a new idea. Porter (1996) emphasized the importance of looking at strategy in this manner and alerted scholars and managers to the importance of fit in strategy. Unfortunately, follow-up research did not build on this idea – but now we have a chance to remedy this. Here lies the uniqueness of the BM construct – it forces us to focus our attention on doing exactly what Porter is suggesting. The business model concept shifts our attention back to this underappreciated concept and can hopefully kick-start a new research programme to explore its importance for strategy. The question that needs to guide our thinking is, 'What new questions emerge for the strategy field as a result of looking at the firm as a system of interrelated activities?'

One example might be the challenge of migrating from one business model to a new one. Since a business model is a system of interrelated activities, changing its business model can be a big challenge for a firm. It is not a matter of replacing ten activities with ten alternatives: these ten activities must be changed and then put back together again into a self-reinforcing mosaic where everything fits together effectively. This can be a challenge for any firm – start-up firm or established firm – but it is obviously a bigger challenge for the established firm. The challenge for a start-up firm is how to put the activities together into a self-reinforcing system. The challenge for the established firm is not only to do this but also to make the transition from one system of reinforcing activities to another. How should a firm make such a transition, and how should it manage this migration journey? This is analogous to changing the tire on your car while still driving on the motorway. Although research in strategy has already explored the question of changing a firm's strategy, there has been no research that explores the migration process by focusing on activities and the need to change one *architecture* to another. This is a new research area for strategy that becomes evident only when we focus on what is unique to the BM construct.

Another example of a research question that emerges when we look at the firm as a system of interrelated activities is the sources of competitive advantage and how a firm can build one. Traditionally, we have looked at the firm's industry position as a source of competitive advantage (Porter, 1980). The positioning view was later supplemented by the resource-based view that emphasized the importance of assets and resources that are difficult to imitate or replicate as sources of competitive advantage (Barney 2001). Looking at the firm through the BM lens – as a system of interconnected activities – alerts us to the fact that a firm's competitive advantage can also emerge from the shape, structure and robustness of its business model (Lanzolla and Markides, 2021). Specifically, the more activities there are that make up a firm's business model, and the more tightly they are interlinked, the more difficult it is for another firm to imitate that business model. The challenge, therefore, is not to simply develop a new BM but to develop one that is 'complex' (Rivkin, 2000). This is the research question that we should be exploring – not 'how to build a new business model' but 'how to build a new business model that is difficult to imitate because it is complex and made up of numerous tightly-knitted activities'.

Developing and adopting such a complex BM will give the firm competitive advantage but it can also create problems. The task is to create a tight system which remains flexible and agile enough to respond to changes in the external environment. The tighter the interconnections in the system, the less flexible and agile the system becomes. How, then, can a firm achieve a tight system and remain agile at the same time? Similarly, the challenge of migrating to a new BM becomes even harder, the tighter the original system is. Our research should be aiming to explore not only how to migrate from one position to another but how the tightness of the original system affects the migration process and the leadership challenges associated with that.

These are just two examples of the types of questions that emerge once we focus our attention on the theoretical differences between the constructs of strategy and of business models. It is not meant to be an exhaustive list – there are many other questions that can be identified. But this is the area where future work on business models ought to focus.

Trade-offs and Conflicts

A second feature that is unique to the intellectual territory of BMI is the presence of trade-offs between the existing BM and the BMI as well as the existence of conflicts between the new market created by BMI and the core market. The presence of trade-offs and conflicts makes BMI a rare type of innovation, namely one that established firms would not want to introduce and would have serious difficulties in responding to. If trade-offs and conflicts are what make BMI such a unique phenomenon, it follows that the most interesting research questions will be those that put trade-offs and conflicts at the centre of their investigation – questions such as 'how to compete with two different and conflicting business models at the same time?' or 'how to respond to disruptive BMI?' This implies that studying BMI within the context of start-up firms will miss out on the most interesting questions to ask. Since a start-up firm does not already have a BM, it would face no trade-offs or conflicts if it were to introduce a BMI. Thus, start-up firms do not have to address some of the most interesting questions within the BMI field.

The presence of trade-offs and conflicts is what makes BMI unpalatable and difficult for established firms. These insights should not come as a surprise to academics familiar with the literature in Economics on rent-displacing innovations or the strategy literature on competence-destroying innovations. However, what we have failed to appreciate is that there are different *types* of trade-offs (such as distribution, culture, incentives, attitudes etc.) as well as different *degrees* of conflict (i.e. minor vs. major). This might sound like an obvious point – but it suggests that not all business model innovations are equally disruptive. Some are more disruptive than others. This, in turn, has two serious implications.

First, one of the most interesting questions in the BMI literature has been that of how an established firm can exploit the market created by a new business model. The perspective taken was that the presence of trade-offs and conflicts makes it difficult for an established firm to exploit the new market without resorting to a separate unit to house the new business model. Unfortunately, this perspective assumes that all new business models are equally disruptive. This is never the case – as we have already said, some business models are more disruptive than others. This implies that the degree of a business model's disruptiveness should determine whether the firm builds the new business model in a separate unit or within its existing organizational infrastructure. Before we develop prescriptions about how a firm ought to compete with dual business models, we need an explicit understanding of how disruptive a new business model actually is. The existing literature has failed to develop such an understanding, because it has taken the concept of 'disruptiveness' as homogeneous.

The same argument could be made regarding the question of how to respond to a disruptive BMI. The dominant way of thinking in the BMI literature was that responding was equivalent to adopting the BMI. However, the level of disruptiveness of the BMI should determine whether adopting it is the optimal response. An alternative response will be for the established firm to focus on its own business model and invest to improve it in ways that allow it to defend effectively against the BMI. Not that the 'level' of disruptiveness is the only factor that should influence the response strategy of the established firm. Which particular trade-off or conflict is creating the disruptiveness of the BMI should also affect what the established firm does. For example, how and what the firm does to respond to a BMI will depend on whether the trade-off between the two business models is a distribution one or an incentive or cultural one. Overall, the point being made here is that a focus on trade-offs and conflicts – a feature unique to BMI – will allow for the identification of research questions that are unique to the BM literature and are ones that have not already been explored in the strategy literature.

Enriching the Business Model Innovation Literature

Identifying the theoretical region where there is no overlap between strategy and BM will help us not only to raise questions that are unique to BMI but also to identify what ideas and theories within the strategy field are relevant and useful to the BMI literature. We can then 'import' these ideas to help us understand the BMI phenomenon better. For example, the literature on *techno-logical innovation* has studied how and why established firms could explore technologies proactively which are both competence- and complementary asset-destroying. This literature could help researchers who are studying how established firms strive to promote disruptive innovations alongside their estab-lished business model. Similarly, the *diversification literature* has studied the concepts of related and unrelated diversification and has explored how synergies between related businesses can be exploited. These insights can help BMI researchers who are exploring how firms can compete by running two business models at the same time. Finally, the *ambidexterity literature* can be a rich source of ideas to understand how established firms can develop disruptive business models, and how to grow them next to their established businesses. The oft-heard statement 'there is nothing new under the sun' applies equally well to the business model literature, and we would do well to look at other literatures to guide the research in this field.

References

Abell, D. F. (1980). *Defining the business: The starting point of strategic planning.* Englewood Cliffs, NJ: Prentice Hall.

Abernathy, W. J. and Utterback, J. (1978). Patterns of industrial innovation. *Technology Review,* 80, 40–7.

Afuah, A. (2003). *Business models: A strategic management approach.* Boston, MA: McGraw-Hill/Irwin.

Afuah, A. and Tucci, C. L. (2001). *Internet business models and strategies: Text and cases.* New York: McGraw Hill.

Agarwal, R., Sarkar, M. B. and Echambadi R. (2002). The conditioning effect of time on firm survival: An industry life cycle approach. *Academy of Management Journal,* 45(5), 971–94.

Amit, R. and Zott, C. (2001). Value creation in e-business. *Strategic Management Journal,* 22(6–7), 493–520.

Amit, R. and Zott, C. (2012). Creating value through business model innovation. *MIT Sloan Management Review,* 53(3), 41–9.

Amit, R. and Zott, C. (2015). Crafting business architecture: The antecedents of business model design. *Strategic Entrepreneurship Journal,* 9(4), 331–50.

Amit, R. and Zott, C. (2021). *Business model innovation strategy: Transformational concepts and tools for entrepreneurial leaders.* Hoboken, NJ: John Wiley & Sons.

Arend, R. (2013). The business model: Present and future – beyond a skeumorph. *Strategic Organization,* 11(4), 390–402.

Atkinson, J. W. (1964). *An introduction to motivation.* Oxford: Van Nostrand.

Audretsch, D. B. (1995). *Innovation and industry evolution.* Cambridge, MA: Massachusetts Institute of Technology Press.

Aversa, P., Furnari, S. and Haefliger, S. (2015). Business model configurations and performance: A qualitative comparative analysis in Formula One racing, 2005–2013. *Industrial and Corporate Change,* 24(3), 655–76.

Aversa, P., Haefliger, S. and Reza, D. G. (2017). Building a winning business model portfolio. *MIT Sloan Management Review,* 58(4), 49–54.

Baden-Fuller, C. and Haefliger, S. (2013). Business models and technological innovation. *Long Range Planning,* 46(6), 419–26.

Baden-Fuller, C. and Mangematin, V. (2013). Business models: A challenging agenda. *Strategic Organization,* 11(4), 418–27.

Baden-Fuller, C. and Morgan, M. (2010). Business models as models. *Long Range Planning,* 43(2–3), 156–71.

Barney, J. B. (1986). Types of competition and the theory of strategy: Toward an integrative framework. *Academy of Management Review*, 11(4), 791–800.

Barney, J. B. (2001). Resource-based theories of competitive advantage: A ten-year retrospective on the resource-based view. *Journal of Management*, 27(6), 643–50.

Bartlett, C. and Ghoshal, S. (1989). *Managing across borders: The transnational solution*. Boston, MA: HBS Press.

Bellman, R., Clark, C. E., Malcolm, D. G., Craft, C. J. and Ricciardi, F. M. (1957). On the construction of a multi-stage, multi-person business game. *Operations Research*, 5(4), 469–503.

Bigelow, L. S. and Barney, J. B. (2021). What can strategy learn from the business model approach? *Journal of Management Studies*, 58(2), 528–39.

Biggadike, R. (1979). The risky business of diversification. *Harvard Business Review*, 57(May), 103–11.

Bock, A. J., Opsahl, T., George, G. and Gann, D. M. (2012). The effects of culture and structure on strategic flexibility during business model innovation. *Journal of Management Studies*, 49(2), 279–305.

Bower, J. and Christensen, C. (1995). Disruptive technologies: Catching the wave. *Harvard Business Review*, 73(1), 43–53.

Bucherer, E., Eisert, U. and Gassmann, O. (2012). Towards systematic business model innovation: Lessons from product innovation management. *Creativity and Innovation Management*, 21(2), 183–98.

Burgelman, R. and Sayles, L. (1986). *Inside corporate innovation*. New York: Free Press.

Casadesus-Masanell, R. and Ricart, J. E. (2010). From strategy to business models and onto tactics. *Long Range Planning*, 43(2–3), 195–215.

Charitou, C. D. (2001). The response of established firms to disruptive strategic innovation: Empirical evidence from Europe and North America. Unpublished doctoral dissertation, London Business School.

Charitou, C. D. and Markides, C. C. (2003). Responses to disruptive strategic innovation. *MIT Sloan Management Review*, 44(2), 55–63.

Chen, M. J. and Miller, D. (1994). Competitive attack, retaliation and performance: An expectancy-valence framework. *Strategic Management Journal*, 15(2), 85–102.

Chen, M. J., Smith, K. G. and Grimm, C. M. (1992). Action characteristics as predictors of competitive responses. *Management Science*, 38(3), 439–55.

Chesbrough, H. (2007). Business model innovation: It's not just about technology anymore. *Strategy & Leadership*, 35(6), 12–17.

Chesbrough, H. (2010). Business model innovation: Opportunities and barriers. *Long Range Planning*, 43(2–3), 354–63.

Chesbrough, H. and Rosenbloom, R. S. (2002). The role of the business model in capturing value from innovation: Evidence from Xerox corporation's technology spin-off companies. *Industrial and Corporate Change*, 11(3), 529–55.

Christensen, C. (1997). *The innovator's dilemma: When new technologies cause great firms to fail*. Boston, MA: Harvard Business School Press.

Christensen, C. M. (2006). The ongoing process of building a theory of disruption. *Journal of Product Innovation Management*, 23(1), 39–55.

Christensen, C. M. and Overdorf, M. (2000). Meeting the challenge of disruptive change. *Harvard Business Review*, 78(2), 67–76.

Christensen, C. M. and Raynor, M. E. (2003). *The innovator's solution: Creating and sustaining successful growth*. Boston, MA: Harvard Business School Press.

Christensen, C. M., Johnson, M. W. and Rigby, D. K. (2002). Foundations for growth: How to identify and build disruptive new businesses. *MIT Sloan Management Review*, 43(3), 22–31.

Cooper, A. C. and Smith, C. G. (1992). How established firms respond to threatening technologies. *Academy of Management Executive*, 6(2), 55–70.

Danneels, E. (2004). Disruptive technology reconsidered: A critique and research agenda. *Journal of Product Innovation Management*, 21(4), 246–58.

Dasilva, C. M. and Trkman, P. (2014). Business model: What is it and what it is not. *Long Range Planning*, 47(6), 379–89.

Day, G. S. and Freeman, J. S. (1990). Burnout or fadeout: The risks of early entry into high technology markets, in M. W. Lawless and L. R. Gomez-Mejia (eds.), *Strategic management in high technology firms*, pp. 43–65, Greenwich, CT: JAI Press Inc.

Day, J., Mang, P. Y., Richter, A. and Roberts, J. (2001). The innovative organization: Why new ventures need more than a room of their own. *The McKinsey Quarterly*, 2, 21.

Demil, B. and Lecocq, X. (2010). Business model evolution: In search of dynamic consistency. *Long Range Planning*, 43(2–3), 227–46.

Doganova, L. and Eyquem-Renault, M. (2009). What do business models do? Innovation devices in technology entrepreneurship. *Research Policy*, 38(10), 1559–70.

Doz, Y. L. and Kosonen, M. (2010). Embedding strategic agility: A leadership agenda for accelerating business model renewal. *Long Range Planning*, 43(2–3), 370–82.

Dunne, T., Roberts, M. and Samuelson, L. (1989). The growth and failure of US manufacturing plants. *Quarterly Journal of Economics*, 104(4), 671–98.

Dutton, J. E. and Jackson, S. E. (1987). Categorizing strategic issues: Links to organizational action. *Academy of Management Review*, 12(1), 76–90.

Foss, N. J. and Saebi, T. (eds.). (2015). *Business model innovation: The organizational dimension*. Oxford: Oxford University Press.

Foss, N. J. and Saebi, T. (2017). Fifteen years of research on business model innovation: How far have we come and where should we go. *Journal of Management*, 43(1), 200–27.

Fuentelsaz, L., Gomez, J. and Polo, Y. (2002). Followers' entry timing: Evidence from the Spanish banking sector after deregulation. *Strategic Management Journal*, 23(3), 245–64.

Gans, J. and Stern, S. (2010). Is there a market for ideas? *Industrial and Corporate Change*, 19(3), 805–37.

Gassmann, O., Frankenberger, K. and Choudury, M. (2020). *The business model navigator: The strategies behind the most successful companies*, 2nd ed. Harlow, UK: FT Pearson.

Gassmann, O., Frankenberger, K. and Sauer, R. (2018). *Exploring the field of business model innovation: New theoretical perspectives*. Basingstoke, UK: Palgrave Macmillan.

Geroski, P. A. (1991). *Market dynamics and entry*. Oxford: Basil Blackwell Ltd

Geroski, P. A. (1995). What do we know about entry? *International Journal of Industrial Organization*, 13(4), 421–40.

Ghoshal, S. and Lynda Gratton (2003). Integrating the enterprise. *MIT Sloan Management Review*, 44(1), 31–8.

Gibson, C. and Birkinshaw, J. (2004). The antecedents, consequences and mediating role of organizational ambidexterity. *Academy of Management Journal*, 47(2), 115–31.

Giesen, E., Berman, S. J., Bell, R. and Blitz, A. (2007). Three ways to successfully innovate your business model. *Strategy & Leadership*, 35(6), 27–33.

Gilbert, C. 2003. The disruption opportunity. *MIT Sloan Management Review*, 44(4), 27–32.

Gilbert, C. and Bower, J. L. (2002). Disruptive change. *Harvard Business Review*, 80(5), 95–100.

Girotra, K. and Netessine, S. (2014). *The risk-driven business model: Four questions that will define your company*. Boston, MA: Harvard Business Press.

Glemet, F. and Mira, R. (1993). The brand leader's dilemma. *McKinsey Quarterly,* 2, 3–15.

Golder, P. and Tellis, G. (1993). Pioneer advantage: Marketing logic or marketing legend? *Journal of Marketing Research*, 30(2), 158–70.

Gomez, J., Lanzolla, G. and Maicas, J. P. (2011). The role of industry dynamics in the sustainability of first movers' advantages. Unpublished manuscript, City Business School, July.

Govindarajan, V. and Trimble, C. (2005). *Ten rules for strategic innovators: From idea to execution.* Boston, MA: HBS Press.

Gulati, R. and Garino, J. (2000). Get the right mix of bricks & clicks. *Harvard Business Review*, 78(3), 107–14.

Gulati, R. and Puranam, P. (2009). Renewal through reorganization: The value of inconsistencies between formal and informal organization. *Organization Science*, 20(2), 422–40.

Günzel, F. and Holm, A. B. (2013). One size does not fit all: Understanding the front-end and back-end of business model innovation. *International Journal of Innovation Management*, 17(01), 1340002.

Hambrick, D. C. and Fredrickson, J. W. (2005). Are you sure you have a strategy? *Academy of Management Perspectives*, 19(4), 51–62.

Hamel, G. (1996). Strategy as revolution. *Harvard Business Review*, 74(4), 69–82.

Hamel, G. (1999). Bringing Silicon Valley inside. *Harvard Business Review*, 77(5), 70–84, 183.

Hamel, G. (2000). Waking up IBM. *Harvard Business Review*, 78(4), 137–44.

Harren, H. (2012). Management of multiple business models: Determining the optimal organizational strategy. Unpublished doctoral dissertation, Technical University of Berlin.

Harren, H., zu Knyphausen-Aufsess, D. and Markides, C. (2022). Managing multiple business models: The role of interdependencies. *Schmalenbach Journal of Business Research*, 74(2), 235–63.

Hedman, J. and Kalling, T. (2003). The business model concept: Theoretical underpinnings and empirical illustrations. *European Journal of Information Systems*, 12(1), 49–59.

House, R. J. (1971). A path goal theory of leader effectiveness. *Administrative Science Quarterly*, 16(3), 321–39.

Iansiti, M., McFarlan, F. W. and Westerman, G. 2003. Leveraging the incumbent's advantage. *MIT Sloan Management Review*, 44(4), 58–64.

Johnson, M. W. and Lafley, A. G. (2010). *Seizing the white space: Business model innovation for growth and renewal.* Boston, MA: Harvard Business Press.

Johnson, M. W., Christensen, C. M. and Kagermann, H. 2008. Reinventing your business model. *Harvard Business Review*, 86(12), 50–9.

Khanagha, S., Volberda, H., Sidhu, J. and Oshri, I. (2013). Management innovation and adoption of emerging technologies. *European Management Review* 10, 51–67.

Kiesler, S. and Sproull, L. (1982). Managerial response to changing environments: Perspectives on problem sensing from social cognition. *Administrative Science Quarterly*, 27, 548–70.

Kim, W. C. and Mauborgne, R. (2005). How to create uncontested market space and make the competition irrelevant. *Harvard Business Review*, 4(13), 1–2.

King, A. A. and Baatartogtokh, B. (2015). How useful is the theory of disruptive innovation? *MIT Sloan Management Review*, 57(1), 77.

Lanzolla, G. and Markides, C. (2021). A business model view of strategy. *Journal Of Management Studies*, 58(2), 540–53.

Laverty, K. J. (1996). Economic 'short-termism': The debate, the unresolved issues, and the implications for management practice and research. *Academy of Management Review*, 21(3), 825–60.

Lieberman, M. and Montgomery, D. (1988). First mover advantages. *Strategic Management Journal*, Special Issue: Strategy Content Research, 9(S1), 41–58.

Lieberman, M. and Montgomery, D. (1998). First-mover (dis)advantages: Retrospective and link with the resource-based view. *Strategic Management Journal*, 19(12), 1111–25.

MacMillan, I., McCaffery, M. L. and Van Wijk, G. (1985). Competitors' responses to easily imitated new products: Exploring commercial banking product introductions. *Strategic Management Journal*, 6(1), 75–86.

Magretta, J. (2002). Why business models matter. *Harvard Business Review*, 80(5), 86–92.

Markides, C. (1997). Strategic innovation. *MIT Sloan Management Review*, 38(3), 9–23.

Markides, C. (1998). Strategic innovation in established companies. *MIT Sloan Management Review*, 39(3), 31–42.

Markides, C. (1999). *All the right moves: A guide to crafting breakthrough strategy*. Boston, MA: Harvard Business School Press.

Markides, C. (2006). Disruptive innovation: In need of better theory. *The Journal of Product Innovation Management*, 23(1), 19–25.

Markides, C. (2008). *Game changing strategies: How to create market space in established industries by breaking the rules*. San Francisco, CA: Jossey-Bass.

Markides, C. (2012). How disruptive will innovations from emerging markets be? *MIT Sloan Management Review*, (54)1, 22–5.

Markides, C. (2013). Business model innovation: What can the ambidexterity literature teach us? *Academy of Management Perspectives*, 27(4), 313–23.

Markides, C. (2015a). How established firms exploit disruptive business model innovation: Strategic and organizational challenges, in N. Foss and T. Saebi (eds.), *Business model innovation: The organizational dimension*, pp. 123–44, Oxford: Oxford University Press.

Markides, C. (2015b). Research on business models: Challenges and opportunities, in C. Baden-Fuller and V. Mangematin (eds.), *Advances in strategic management: Business models and organizations*, pp. 133–47, Bingley, UK: Emerald Group Publishing Ltd.

Markides, C. C. (2021). *Organizing for the new normal: Prepare your company for the journey of continuous disruption*. London: Kogan Page Publishers.

Markides, C. C. and Charitou, C. D. (2004). Competing with dual business models: A contingency approach. *Academy of Management Perspectives* 18(3), 22–36.

Markides, C. and Geroski, P. (2005). *Fast second: How smart companies bypass radical innovation to enter and dominate new markets*. San Francisco. CA: Jossey-Bass.

Markides, C. and Oyon, D. (2000). Changing the strategy at Nespresso: An interview with former CEO Jean-Paul Gaillard. *European Management Journal*, 18(3), 296–301.

Markides, C. C. and Oyon, D. (2010). What to do against disruptive business models: When and how to play two games at once. *MIT Sloan Management Review*, 51(4), 25–32.

Markides, C. and Sosa, L. (2013). Pioneering and first-mover advantages: The importance of business models. *Long Range Planning*, 46(4–5), 325–34.

Markides, C., Larsen, E. and Gary, S. (2020). Business model innovation and the evolution of industry profitability. Working paper, London Business School.

Massa, L. and Tucci, C. (2013). Business model innovation, in M. Dodgson, D. M. Gann and N. Phillips (eds.), *The Oxford handbook of innovation management*, 420–41, Oxford: Oxford University Press.

Massa, L., Tucci, C. and Afuah, A. 2017. A critical assessment of business model research. *Academy of Management Annals*, 11(1), 73–104.

McGrath, R. G. (2010): Business models: A discovery driven approach. *Long Range Planning*, 43(2–3), 247–61.

Mitchell, D. and Coles, C. (2003). The ultimate competitive advantage of continuing business model innovation. *Journal of Business Strategy*, 24(5), 15–21.

Mitchell, D. and Coles, C. (2004). Business model innovation breakthrough moves. *Journal of Business Strategy*, 25(1), 16–26.

Mueller, D. (1997). First-mover advantages and path dependence. *International Journal of Industrial Organization*, 15(6), 827–50.

Newman, A., Obschonka, M., Moeller, J. and Chandan, G. G. (2021). Entrepreneurial passion: A review, synthesis, and agenda for future research. *Applied Psychology*, 70(2), 816–60.

Nickerson, J. A. and Zenger, T. R. (2002). Being efficiently fickle: A dynamic theory of organizational choice. *Organization Science*, 13(5), 547–66.

O'Reilly III, C. A. and Tushman, M. L. 2004. The ambidextrous organization. *Harvard Business Review*, 82(4), 74–81.

O'Reilly III, C. A. and Tushman, M. (2011). Organizational ambidexterity in action: How managers explore and exploit. *California Management*, 53(4), 5–22.

Osterwalder, A. and Pigneur, Y. (2010). *Business model generation: A handbook for visionaries, game changers, and challengers*. Hoboken, NJ: John Wiley & Sons.

Porter, M. E. (1980). *Competitive strategy: Techniques for analyzing industries and competitors*. New York: The Free Press.

Porter, M. E. (1985). *Competitive advantage*. New York: Free Press.

Porter, M. E. (1996). What is strategy? *Harvard Business Review*, 74(6), 61–78.

Porter, M. E. (2001). Strategy and the Internet. *Harvard Business Review*, 79(3), 62–78.

Porter, M. and Siggelkow, N. (2008). Contextuality within activity systems and sustainability of competitive advantage. *Academy of Management Perspectives*, 22(2), 34–56.

Puranam, P., Singh, H. and Zollo, M. (2006). Organizing for innovation. *Academy of Management Journal*, 49, 263–80.

Raisch, S. and Birkinshaw, J. (2008). Organizational ambidexterity: Antecedents, outcomes, and moderators. *Journal of Management*, 34(3), 375–409.

Ramdani, B., Binsaif, A. and Boukrami, E. (2019). Business model innovation: A review and research agenda. *New England Journal of Entrepreneurship*, 22(2), 89–108.

Rivkin, J. W. (2000). Imitation of complex strategies. *Management Science*, 46(6), 824–44.

Rivkin, J. W. and Siggelkow, N. (2003). Balancing search and stability: Interdependencies among elements of organizational design. *Management Science*, 49(3), 290–311.

Robinson, W. and Chiang, J. (2002). Product development strategies for established market pioneers, early followers and late entrants. *Strategic Management Journal*, 23(9), 855–66.

Santos, J., Spector, B. and Van der Heyden, L. (2009). Toward a theory of business model innovation within incumbent firms. INSEAD Working Paper No. 2009/16/EFE/ST/TOM, accessed at SSRN: https://ssrn.com/abstract=1362515 or http://dx.doi.org/10.2139/ssrn.1362515.

Schnaars, S. (1994). *Managing imitation strategies*. New York: The Free Press.

Schneider, S. and Spieth, P. (2013). Business model innovation: Towards an integrated future research agenda. *International Journal of Innovation Management*, 17(1), 1340001.

Schumpeter, J. A. (1942). *Capitalism, Socialism and Democracy.*

Seddon, P. B., Lewis, G. P., Freeman, P. and Shanks, G. (2004). The case for viewing business models as abstractions of strategy. *Communications of the Association for Information Systems*, 13(1), 25.

Senge, P. M. (1990). *The art and practice of the learning organization* (Vol. 1). New York: Doubleday.

Shankar, V., Carpenter, G. and Krishnamurthi, L. (1998). Late mover advantage: How innovative late entrants outsell pioneers. *Journal of Marketing Research*, 35(1), 54–70.

Siggelkow, N. (2001). Change in the Presence of Fit: The Rise, The Fall, and the Renaissance of Liz Clairborne. *Academy of Management Journal*, 44, 838-857.

Siggelkow, N. (2017). Change in the presence of fit: The rise, the fall, and the renaissance of Liz Claiborne, in B. Chakravarthy, G. Mueller-Stevens, P. Lorange and C. Lechner (eds.), *Strategy process*, pp. 45–73, Oxford: Blackwell Publishing Ltd.

Siggelkow, N. and Levinthal, D. (2003). Temporarily divide to conquer: Centralized, decentralized and reintegrated organizational approaches to exploration and adaptation. *Organization Science*, 14(6), 650–76.

Sinfield, J. V., Calder, E., McConnell, B. and Colson, S. (2012). How to identify new business models. *MIT Sloan Management Review*, 53(2), 85–90.

Slywotzky, A. J. (1996). *Value migration: How to think several moves ahead of the competition.* Boston: HBS Press.

Slywotzky, A. J. and Morrison, D. (2002). *The profit zone.* New York: Three Rivers Press.

Smith, K. G., Grimm, C. M., Gannon, M. J. and Chen, M. J. (1991). Organizational information processing, competitive responses, and performance in the US domestic airline industry. *Academy of Management Journal*, 34(1), 60–85.

Smith, W. K., Binns, A. and Tushman, M. L. (2010). Complex business models: Managing strategic paradoxes simultaneously. *Long Range Planning*, 43(2–3), 448–61.

Snihur, Y. and Tarziján, J. (2018). Managing complexity in a multi-business model organization. *Long Range Planning*, 51(1), 50–63.

Snihur, Y. and Zott, C. (2020). The genesis and metamorphosis of novelty imprints: How business model innovation emerges in young ventures. *Academy of Management Journal*, 63(2), 554–83.

Sohl, T. and Vroom, G. (2017). Mergers and acquisitions revisited: The role of business model relatedness. In *Advances in Mergers and Acquisitions (Advances in Mergers and Acquisitions, Vol. 16)*, pp. 99–113, Bingley, UK: Emerald Publishing Limited. DOI: https://doi.org/10.1108/S1479-361X201700000 16006.

Spieth, P., Schneckenberg D. and Ricart, J. E. (2014). Business model innovation: State of the art and future challenges for the field. *R&D Management*, 44(3), 237–47.

Suarez, F. and Lanzolla, G. (2007). The role of environmental dynamics in building a first mover advantage theory. *Academy of Management Review*, 32(2), 377–92.

Szymanski, D. M., Try, L. C. and Bharadwaj, S. G. (1995). Order of entry and business performance: An empirical synthesis and reexamination. *Journal of Marketing*, 59(4), 17–33.

Teece, D. J. (1986). Profiting from technological innovation: Implications for integration, collaboration, licensing and public policy. *Research Policy*, 15(6), 285–305.

Teece, D. J. (2010). Business models, business strategy and innovation. *Long Range Planning*, 43(2–3), 172–94.

Teece, D. J. (2018). Business models and dynamic capabilities. *Long Range Planning*, 51(1), 40–9.

Teece, D., Pisano, G. and Shuen, A. (1997). Dynamic capabilities and strategic management. *Strategic Management Journal*, 18(7), 509–33.

Tellis, G. and Golder, P. (1996). First to market, first to fail? Real causes of enduring market leadership. *MIT Sloan Management Review*, 37(4), 65–75.

Tellis, G. and Golder, P. (2001). *Will and vision: How latecomers grow to dominate markets*. New York: McGraw Hill.

Thompson, J. D. (1967). *Organizations in action*. New York: McGraw Hill.

Tushman, M. L. and O'Reilly III, C. A. (1996). Ambidextrous organizations: Managing evolutionary and revolutionary change. *California Management Review*, 38(4), 8–30.

Utterback, J. (1996). *Mastering the dynamics of innovation*. Boston: HBS Press.

VanderWerf, P. and Mahon, J. (1997). Meta-analysis of the impact of research methods on findings of first-mover advantage. *Management Science*, 43(11), 1510–19.

Visnjic, I., Wiengarten, F. and Neely, A. (2016). Only the brave: Product innovation, service business model innovation, and their impact on performance. *Journal of Product Innovation Management*, 33(1), 36–52.

Volberda, H. W., Khanagha, S., Sidhu, J. S. and Oshri, I. (2013). Management innovation, absorptive capacity and the adoption of emerging technologies: The case of cloud computing. *European Management Review*, 10(1), 51–67.

Vroom, V. H. (1964). *Work and motivation*. Oxford: Wiley.

Watts, R. M. (2001). *The slingshot syndrome: Why America's leading technology firms fail at innovation*. Lincoln, NE: Writers Club Press.

Wernerfelt, B. (1984). A resource-based view of the firm. *Strategic Management Journal*, 5(2), 171–80.

Zhang, S. and Markman, A. (1998): Overcoming the early entrant advantage: The role of alignable and nonalignable differences. *Journal of Marketing Research*, 35(4), 413–26.

Zott, C. and Amit, R. (2007). Business model design and the performance of entrepreneurial firms. *Organization Science*, 18(2), 181–99.

Zott, C. and Amit, R. (2010). Business model design: An activity system perspective. *Long Range Planning*, 43(2–3), 216–26.

Zott, C. and Amit, R. (2013). The business model: A theoretically anchored robust construct for strategic analysis. *Strategic Organization*, 11(4), 403–11.

Zott, C., Amit, R. and Massa, L. (2011). The business model: Recent developments and future research. *Journal of Management*, 37(4), 1019–42.

Cambridge Elements ≡

Business Strategy

J.-C. Spender
Kozminski University

J.-C. Spender is a research Professor, Kozminski University. He has been active in the business strategy field since 1971 and is the author or co-author of 7 books and numerous papers. His principal academic interest is in knowledge-based theories of the private sector firm, and managing them.

About the Series

Business strategy's reach is vast, and important too since wherever there is business activity there is strategizing. As a field, strategy has a long history from medieval and colonial times to today's developed and developing economies. This series offers a place for interesting and illuminating research including industry and corporate studies, strategizing in service industries, the arts, the public sector, and the new forms of Internet-based commerce. It also covers today's expanding gamut of analytic techniques.

Cambridge Elements ☰

Business Strategy

A full series listing is available at: www.cambridge.org/EBUS

Printed in the United States
by Baker & Taylor Publisher Services

Printed in the United States
by Baker & Taylor Publisher Services